Biography Today

*Profiles
of People
of Interest
to Young
Readers*

Volume 18
Issue 2
April 2009

Cherie D. Abbey
Managing Editor

*P.O. Box 31-1640
Detroit, MI 48231-1640*

Cherie D. Abbey, *Managing Editor*

Brian Baughan, Peggy Daniels, Joan Goldsworthy, Jeff Hill, Kevin Hillstrom, Laurie Hillstrom, and Diane Telgen, *Sketch Writers*

Allison A. Beckett and Mary Butler, *Research Staff*

* * *

Peter E. Ruffner, *Publisher*
Matthew P. Barbour, *Senior Vice President*

* * *

Elizabeth Collins, *Research and Permissions Coordinator*
Kevin M. Hayes, *Operations Manager*
Cherry Stockdale, *Permissions Assistant*

Shirley Amore, Martha Johns, and Kirk Kauffman, *Administrative Staff*

Special thanks to Frederick G. Ruffner for creating this series.

Library of Congress Cataloging-in-Publication Data

Contents

3

Preface

Biography Today is a magazine designed and written for the young reader—ages 9 and above—and covers individuals that librarians and teachers tell us that young people want to know about most: entertainers, athletes, writers, illustrators, cartoonists, and political leaders.

The Plan of the Work

The publication was especially created to appeal to young readers in a format they can enjoy reading and readily understand. Each issue contains approximately 10 sketches arranged alphabetically. Each entry provides at least one picture of the individual profiled, and bold-faced rubrics lead the reader to information on birth, youth, early memories, education, first jobs, marriage and family, career highlights, memorable experiences, hobbies, and honors and awards. Each of the entries ends with a list of easily accessible sources designed to lead the student to further reading on the individual and a current address. Retrospective entries are also included, written to provide a perspective on the individual's entire career.

Biographies are prepared by Omnigraphics editors after extensive research, utilizing the most current materials available. Those sources that are generally available to students appear in the list of further reading at the end of the sketch.

Indexes

Cumulative indexes are an important component of *Biography Today*. Each issue of the *Biography Today* General Series includes a Cumulative Names Index, which comprises all individuals profiled in *Biography Today* since the series began in 1992. In addition, we compile three other indexes: the Cumulative General Index, Places of Birth Index, and Birthday Index. See our web site, www.biographytoday.com, for these three indexes, along with the Names Index. All *Biography Today* indexes are cumulative, including all individuals profiled in both the General Series and the Subject Series.

Our Advisors

This series was reviewed by an Advisory Board comprising librarians, children's literature specialists, and reading instructors to ensure that the concept of this publication—to provide a readable and accessible biographical magazine for young readers—was on target. They evaluated the title as it developed, and their suggestions have proved invaluable. Any errors, however, are ours alone. We'd like to list the Advisory Board members, and to thank them for their efforts.

Our Advisory Board stressed to us that we should not shy away from controversial or unconventional people in our profiles, and we have tried to follow their advice. The Advisory Board also mentioned that the sketches might be useful in reluctant reader and adult literacy programs, and we would value any comments librarians might have about the suitability of our magazine for those purposes.

Your Comments Are Welcome

Our goal is to be accurate and up-to-date, to give young readers information they can learn from and enjoy. Now we want to know what you think. Take a look at this issue of *Biography Today*, on approval, and send me your comments. We want to provide an excellent source of biographical information for young people. Let us know how you think we're doing.

Cherie Abbey
Managing Editor, *Biography Today*
Omnigraphics, Inc.
P.O. Box 31-1640
Detroit, MI 48231-1640
www.omnigraphics.com
editorial@omnigraphics.com

Congratulations!

Congratulations to the following individuals and libraries who are receiving a free copy of *Biography Today,* Vol. 18, No. 2, for suggesting people who appear in this issue.

Susannah Chase, Englewood High School, Jacksonville, FL

Judi Chelekis, Vassar Junior/Senior High School, Vassar, MI

Elizabeth Alexander 1962-

American Poet and Professor
Featured Poet at the Inauguration of President
Barack Obama

EARLY YEARS

Elizabeth Alexander was born on May 30, 1962, in Harlem, a section of New York City. Her father, Clifford Alexander, was a civil rights advisor to President Lyndon B. Johnson and also became the first African-American Secretary of the Army. Later he established his own political consulting business. Her mother, Adele Alexander, was a writer and professor who became professor of African-American women's history at

George Washington University. The family also included a younger brother, Mark, a professor of constitutional law and politics who served as an advisor to Barack Obama during his presidential campaign.

Alexander's parents moved to Washington DC shortly after her birth. She was just a toddler when her parents brought her to the 1963 March on Washington. Although she doesn't remember any of it, she was a witness to Martin Luther King Jr.'s famous "I Have a Dream" speech. Her family was dedicated to the causes of civil rights and public service. "[Politics] was in the drinking water in my house," she recalled. Education was important, but so were the arts. "I grew up taking ballet," Alexander revealed. "Very seriously and quite regularly. I think that listening to music and trying to learn how to make my body do things with music and trying to be, as our teachers would say, sensitive to the music, have a lot to do with trying to have and utilize an ear in poetry." She was also fascinated by words and the way people spoke. She had family from Alabama, Jamaica, and New York City, and they could "tell you [the same thing] in such different ways," she said. "I was intrigued that there were so many variations and possibilities in the language."

EDUCATION

Alexander went to Sidwell Friends School, the private school in Washington DC attended by many children of prominent politicians, including the daughters of President Barack Obama. She graduated in 1980 and entered Yale University, where she received a Bachelor of Arts (BA) degree in 1984. She studied poetry at Boston University under Nobel Prize-winning poet Derek Walcott and received her Master of Arts (MA) degree in 1987. She received a doctorate (PhD) in English from the University of Pennsylvania in 1992.

MAJOR ACCOMPLISHMENTS

Becoming a Poet and Professor

Although Alexander would become famous worldwide for the poem she composed for President Barack Obama's inauguration, she didn't graduate from Yale intending to become a poet. She worked as a reporter for the *Washington Post* from 1984 to 1985 before realizing "it wasn't the life I wanted," she recalled. "My mother said, 'That poet you love, Derek Walcott, is teaching at Boston University. Why don't you apply." Alexander entered the program to study fiction writing, but Walcott looked at her diary and showed her the poetry within. "He gave me a huge gift," the author said. "He took a cluster of words and he lineated it. And I saw it." At this

Miss Crandall's School for Young Ladies, *a book of poetry that Alexander co-wrote with Marilyn Nelson, was her first book for young readers.*

time she also discovered a love for teaching and began working towards a career as a professor.

While she was finishing her doctoral degree (PhD) at the University of Pennsylvania, Alexander taught at nearby Haverford College from 1990 to 1991. In 1991 she also published her first poetry collection, titled *The Venus Hottentot*. The title poem is from the point of view of Sarah Baartman, a 19th-century South African woman of the Khoikhoi ethnic group. Baartman agreed to travel to Europe as part of a traveling exhibit so that people could marvel at the shape of her buttocks, which were unusually large but normal for her tribe. In other portions of the book Alexander writes about her family and some of her artistic heroes. Reviewing the collection in *Poetry* magazine, Stephen Yenser remarked, "I am sure, or as sure as I can be, that it will be a landmark in American poetry, and that *The Venus Hottentot* is a superb first book, and that Elizabeth Alexander can be about as good a poet as she cares to be."

Alexander began teaching at the University of Chicago in 1991, serving as an assistant professor of English. There she first met Barack Obama, who was a senior lecturer at the university's law school from 1992 until his election to the U.S. Senate in 2004. She lived near Obama and his wife, Michelle, and introduced them to her brother,

Mark, a law professor who later worked on Obama's presidential campaign and transition team.

Alexander continued growing as a writer while in Chicago. In 1992 she won a creative writing fellowship from the National Endowment for the Arts, and in 1996 she produced both a volume of poetry, *Body of Life,* and a verse play, *Diva Studies,* which was staged at Yale University. Alexander also continued to advance her academic career during this time. In 1996 she became a founding faculty member of the *Cave Canem* workshop, which helps develop African-American poets. The following year she received the University of Chicago's Quantrell Award for Excellence in Undergraduate Teaching. In 1997 Alexander moved to Massachusetts to work at Smith College, one of the country's most prestigious women's colleges. She served as the Grace Hazard Conkling Poet-in-Residence and became the first director of the college's Poetry Center.

In 2000 Alexander returned to Yale University, where she became a professor in African-American studies and English. The following year she published a third poetry collection, *Antebellum Dream Book.* Her poems once again explored topics that were personal, popular, and historical. In some poems she remembers growing up in the civil rights movement; in others she imagines interacting with novelist Toni Morrison, basketball player Michael Jordan, singer Nat King Cole, and comedian Richard Pryor. The poem "Narrative: Ali" imagines the voice of boxing legend Muhammad Ali. According to Jace Clayton, a critic for the *Washington Post,* the collection "sports the page-turning pull of a good story, the intimacy of personal verse, and an unforced braininess that so few smart poets can get right."

Developing as a Writer

Alexander continued developing her reputation as a poet and scholar in the new century. She won a Guggenheim Foundation fellowship in 2002 and published her first collection of essays in 2004. A *Booklist* reviewer called *The Black Interior* an "original and electrifying collection [that] greatly enriches and extends understanding of African-American culture and its essential role in American culture as a whole." In 2005 she won one of the first Alphonse Fletcher Sr. fellowships, a $50,000 award supporting people who further the goals of civil rights and racial understanding. That same year she published another book of poetry, *American Sublime.* It was another combination of personal and historical themes, with one section in particular exploring the true story of the slave ship *Amistad.* In 1839, more than 50 African captives took control of *Amistad* as it sailed from Cuba to America and successfully won their freedom in a Connecticut court. *American Sublime* was a finalist for the 2005 Pulitzer Prize in Poetry.

Alexander explained her fascination with using American and especially African-American history in her poems: "Our history is so rich, but there are so many stories within it that haven't yet been told, or have been improperly told, or that can yield something particular when explored through poetry." One such story can be found in Alexander's first poetry collection for young readers, written with Marilyn Nelson and published in 2007. *Miss Crandall's School for Young Ladies and Little Misses of Color* is based on the true story of Prudence Crandall, a Connecticut school teacher who opened the first school for African-American girls in New England. Through 24 poems—all in sonnet form—Alexander and Nelson give the students voice as they relate how their school is shunned and eventually destroyed by racial hatred.

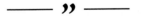

By 2008, Alexander had achieved renown as a poet and professor. In 2007 she had published a second volume of essays, *Power and Possibility*, and received the first $50,000 Jackson Poetry Prize. This award recognizes a poet who has published at least one book of poems but has not received "major national acclaim."

"I continue to advocate for the necessity of the arts in everybody's day-to-day life," Alexander asserted. *"If [the inaugural poem] means those things that I'm trained to talk about will get more hearing, that would be fantastic."*

An Inaugural Honor

In 2008, Barack Obama was elected the 44th President of the United States. At that time, Alexander was not widely known outside of academic circles, but then the president-elect selected her to write a poem to be read at his inauguration. She was thrilled that President Obama had commissioned her to write a poem. "I think that he is showing that moments of pause and contemplation in the midst of grand occasion and everyday life are necessary," she said.

Alexander believed she was chosen not because of her friendship with Obama—he and his wife know several poets—but because of her voice. To be chosen to read at the inauguration made her feel "very, very, very humble," although she wasn't scared of having to read in front of an estimated audience of two million people. "Not only is the audience enormous, but unimaginably diverse," she explained. "Paradoxically what is freeing is

13

Alexander reciting her poem, "Praise Song for the Day,"
at the 2009 inauguration of President Barack Obama.

when you really don't know [the audience], you have to listen to and trust your own voice." Poet Maya Angelou, one of only three other poets to read at a presidential inauguration, expressed confidence in the selection of Alexander: "She seems much like Walt Whitman," Angelou told the *New York Times*. "She sings the American song."

On January 20, 2009, Alexander shared the stage with the newly inaugurated President Obama and read her 341-word poem, "Praise Song for the Day." Her poem spoke of everyday American lives, the sacrifices that led to this historic moment, and the power of language: "We encounter each other in words, words/ spiny or smooth, whispered or declaimed;/ words to consider, reconsider." Her concluding lines reflected the sense of hope and inspiration many felt on the occasion: "In today's sharp sparkle, this winter air,/ any thing can be made, any sentence begun./ On the brink, on the brim, on the cusp,/ praise song for walking forward in that light."

Readers around the world critiqued Alexander's poem—some found it too prosaic, others thought it suited to the occasion—but what mattered to Alexander was the visibility her

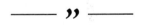

"Words matter. Language matters. We live in and express ourselves with language, and that is how we communicate and move through the world in community," Alexander explained. "Poetry is not meant to cheer; rather, poetry challenges.... Language distilled and artfully arranged shifts our experience of the words—and the worldviews—we live in."

role on Inauguration Day gave to her work and literature in general. "I continue to advocate for the necessity of the arts in everybody's day-to-day life," she asserted. "If [the inaugural poem] means those things that I'm trained to talk about will get more hearing, that would be fantastic." In addition, she looked forward to becoming chairperson of Yale's African American Studies department beginning in summer 2009, and bringing poetry to more people. "Words matter. Language matters. We live in and express ourselves with language, and that is how we communicate and move through the world in community," she explained. "Poetry is not meant to cheer; rather, poetry challenges, and moves us towards transformation. Language distilled and artfully arranged shifts our experience of the words—and the worldviews—we live in."

MARRIAGE AND FAMILY

Alexander married Gustavo A. Paredes, a salesman, on September 18, 1993. They have two sons and live in the New Haven, Connecticut, area.

SELECTED WRITINGS

The Venus Hottentot, 1990 (poetry)
Body of Life, 1996 (poetry)
Diva Studies, 1996 (play in verse)
Antebellum Dream Book, 2001 (poetry)
The Black Interior, 2004 (essays)
American Sublime, 2005 (poetry)
Miss Crandall's School for Young Ladies and Little Misses of Color, 2007
   (young adult poetry, with Marilyn Nelson)
Power and Possibility, 2007 (essays)
"Praise Song for the Day," 2009 (inaugural poem)

HONORS AND AWARDS

George Kent Prize (*Poetry* magazine): 1992, 1997
Pushcart Prize for Poetry (Pushcart Press): 1998, 2000, 2001
Guggenheim Foundation Fellowship: 2002
Alphonse Fletcher Sr. Fellowship: 2005
Jackson Poetry Prize (Poets & Writers): 2007

FURTHER READING

Periodicals

Booklist, Jan. 1, 2004, p.794
New York Times, Dec. 21, 2008; Dec. 25, 2008, p.C1; Jan. 18, 2009, p.CT5
New York Times Book Review, Sep. 30, 1990
Poetry, July 1991, p.214
Radcliffe Quarterly, Summer 2008
Wall Street Journal, Dec. 20, 2008, p.W4
Washington Post, Oct. 21, 2001, p.T13; Dec. 18, 2008, p.A1; Jan. 21, 2009,
   p.C10

Online Articles

http://www.pbs.org/newshour/bb/entertainment/jan-june09/inaug_poet
   _01-13.html
   (PBS.org, "Poet Elizabeth Alexander Reflects on Inaugural Reading,"
   Jan. 13, 2009)

http://www.poetryfoundation.org/archive/poet.html?id=84
   (Poetry Foundation, "Elizabeth Alexander, 1962-)," 2009)
http://www.time.com/time/arts/article/0,8599,1872643,00.html
   (Time.com, "Q&A: Inauguration Poet Elizabeth Alexander," Jan. 20,
   2009)

ADDRESS

Elizabeth Alexander
Department of African American Studies
Yale University
81 Wall Street
New Haven, CT 06510

WORLD WIDE WEB SITE

http://www.elizabethalexander.net

Michael Cera 1988-

Canadian Actor
Star of *Superbad, Juno,* and *Nick & Norah's Infinite Playlist*

BIRTH

Michael Austin Cera was born on June 7, 1988, in the Canadian town of Brampton, Ontario. He is the son of Luigi and Linda Cera, both of whom worked for Xerox at the time of his birth. Michael is the second of three children and has an older sister named Jordan and a younger sister named Molly.

YOUTH

Cera grew up in Brampton, which is a suburb of Toronto. While still quite young, he began to display an offbeat sense of humor that made an impression on his parents. "He never connected with the over-the-top humor that usually made other kids laugh, making faces and stupid dances and things," said Linda Cera. "But if I'd knock my arm into the furniture and pretend I was hurt, that made him laugh." Overall, Cera's personality was more laid-back than outgoing, and his mother noted that "he wasn't ever the one hamming it up for attention."

——— *"* ———

"He never connected with the over-the-top humor that usually made other kids laugh, making faces and stupid dances and things," said Linda Cera. "But if I'd knock my arm into the furniture and pretend I was hurt, that made him laugh."

——— *"* ———

Though he may have been reserved in some ways, Cera became interested in acting at a very young age. He was initially inspired by the movie *Ghostbusters*, which he watched over and over when he was sick with the chicken pox at age three. Soon after, he had all of the film's dialog memorized and was especially enthralled with star Bill Murray, who has remained one of his idols. Around this time, he informed his parents of his future plans: he was going to be an actor.

EDUCATION

Responding to his interest, his parents enrolled him in drama classes, and he soon showed enough promise that he was advised to seek out an agent. Cera studied various approaches in honing his dramatic skills. One of them was improvisational acting, which he learned in classes with the Second City comedy troupe in Toronto. This approach involves making up dialog for characters on the spur of the moment rather than reciting lines from a script, and Cera later put this approach to use in some of his films. He also learned by immersing himself in his favorite television comedies, which included "Mr. Show" and "The Tom Green Show."

Meanwhile, there was general schoolwork to attend to. Initially, Cera was educated in Brampton-area public schools, including Heart Lake Secondary School. But as his career gained steam, he completed independent studies and worked with a tutor, and he eventually earned his diploma in that manner. His last full year in a regular school took place when he was in 10th grade—his initial year of high school. "I never got to have anyone below me in high school," he later explained. "I never got to be on top.... Maybe that's good. It shaped who I was. I wasn't ever able to look at people as beneath me."

Even while he was attending a regular school, Cera was somewhat of an outsider, though he sometimes deliberately chose to be "uncool" just for the fun of it. Reflecting on his experiences as a seventh grader, he recalled that "there was a day when my friend Chris and I decided we didn't care what people thought of us." To prove that point, he began wearing a pink bicycle helmet and unusual clothing to school. "I decided to start wearing the helmet and see if people thought I was an idiot," he said. "And then I was excited about people thinking I was an idiot." Cera's interest in uncomfortable circumstances has extended to more recent times as well. "I always kind of end up in situations where I don't know too many people," he explained, "and I'm not very social, and I feel, you know, extremely uncomfortable. But there's some secret pleasure I take in things like that, in things going horribly wrong."

CAREER HIGHLIGHTS

Cera's professional career began when he was nine years old. His first job was in a television commercial for Tim Hortons, a popular coffee-and-doughnuts chain that started in Canada and has since expanded into the United States. Another commercial for Pillsbury followed, but this success was short-lived. He was turned down for some 200 other roles in advertising before deciding to focus on dramatic roles. His first job in that field came in 1998, when he provided the voice of Little Gizmo in the Disney Channel animated program "Rolie Polie Olie," and he later undertook voice work for other cartoons. On-camera roles began in 1999 with his part in "I Was a Sixth-Grade Alien" on the Canadian YTV channel, and he also appeared in several made-for-television movies.

In 2000, Cera made the jump to the big screen, and his early film work included supporting roles in *Frequency, Steal This Movie,* and *Confessions of a Dangerous Mind.* During this period, he and his mother began spending time in the Los Angeles area so that he would have more opportunities to audition for roles. In the years since, he has regularly resided in California for certain periods, though the family home in Brampton continues to be his permanent home base.

In 2002, Cera was cast in "The Grubbs," a new Fox television series. Five episodes were produced, but the show proved to be his introduction to the uncertain nature of TV work. Advance screenings of the series received a very poor response, including an E! Online review that called it "the worst

Scenes from Cera's career: "Rolie Polie Olie," "Arrested Development," and "Clark and Michael."

sitcom ever produced." As a result, the network decided to cancel "The Grubbs" before it ever aired. Cera then landed a role doing the voice of Brother Bear on the cartoon series "The Berenstain Bears." After that, he was cast in another Fox series, "Arrested Development." Unlike his experience with "The Grubbs," his performance in this new series not only made it to the airwaves, it provided the launching pad for his later acting success.

"Arrested Development"

The new series was a situation comedy entitled "Arrested Development." When he read the script, Cera was excited by the mock-documentary style and by the offbeat storylines, which relay the comic adventures of a formerly wealthy family that has fallen on hard times. Cera auditioned for the role of George Michael Bluth—the 13-year-old son of the show's main protagonist—and was one of the first actors cast in the show. When "Arrested Development" hit the airwaves in 2003, his portrayal of the gawky George Michael, who develops a crush on his cousin, was one of the highlights that impressed critics.

In fact, reviewers liked almost everything about the program, particularly its quirky and sophisticated humor. In 2004, "Arrested Development" earned six Emmy Awards and a TV Land Award, and the cast was nominated for Screen Actors Guild awards in two consecutive years. Unfortunately, the official honors and critical praise did not translate into high ratings, and the show was cancelled in 2006, much to the disappointment of its small but devoted audience. Nonetheless, "Arrested Development" provided Cera with valuable acting experience, and his performance as George Michael gave him a much higher profile in the entertainment industry. Mitchell Hurwitz, the creator of "Arrested Development," was one of those who recognized that Cera was destined for further success. "He just has this uncanny maturity," Hurwitz explained in 2007, "and I think he's going to be a big part of this next generation of comic actors."

"Arrested Development" also proved important because it allowed Cera his first substantial opportunity to depict a confused adolescent character, and such roles have become the mainstay of his career to date. His George Michael Bluth character became famous for delivering a high-pitched laugh that indicates his uneasiness. In addition, Cera's work in "Arrested Development" and later projects demonstrated his skill in creating awkward silences that allow the viewer to experience some of the self-conscious embarrassment that is felt by the characters he plays.

Cera had the opportunity to explore dramatic disasters in greater detail when he collaborated with his friend Clark Duke on the Internet-only series "Clark and Michael." At that time, in 2005, Duke was enrolled in film school at Loyola Marymount University. The "Clark and Michael" show began as a project for his film-school studies and expanded into 10 episodes of about 10 minutes each. Utilizing the "mockumentary" approach, "Clark and Michael" relays the mishaps of two inept screenwriters who try to convince Hollywood executives to produce a script they have written. Cera and Duke wrote the screenplay as well as serving as the program's stars, and the episodes demonstrate the dry sense of humor that Cera frequently exhibits when not playing movie roles. The series was sold to CBS, and in 2007, it became one of the network's first scripted online video shows, available on the "Clark and Michael" web site.

Cera has had a hand in several other short comic video segments that have become popular on sites such as YouTube. He wrote and starred in "Impossible is the Opposite of Possible," an offbeat spoof of a real-life video resume, and had a role in an episode of "Drunk History." In addition, he was part of a short comedy piece related to the film *Knocked Up*, appearing as an actor who gets into a shouting match with the film's director, Judd Apatow, during a screen test. The mock audition was included as an extra feature on the DVD release of the movie.

Superbad

The *Knocked Up* comic segment proved to be just one of Cera's projects with Apatow. Their larger collaboration was the 2007 film *Superbad*, in which Cera delivered a breakout performance in his first leading role in a motion picture. The comedy follows two high school seniors, Evan and Seth—played by Cera and costar Jonah Hill—over the course of a very eventful 24-hour period shortly before graduation. Up to this point in their lives, the two have not enjoyed much success with the opposite sex, but they see an opportunity to change their status when a popular female classmate invites them to a party. The catch is, they need to supply alcohol for the underage party-goers, which launches the duo and their friend Fogell into a series of adventures that involve a fake ID, stolen liquor, and numerous run-ins with two less-than-upstanding police officers.

Produced by Apatow and written by Seth Rogen and Evan Goldberg, *Superbad* features many of the film elements often associated with Apatow's work, including raunchy situations, off-color humor, and lots of profane language. Most critics took the crudeness in stride, however, and appreciated the film's realistic portrayal of teen dialog and preoccupations. Moreover, Cera and his costars frequently received high marks for their honest

Christopher Mintz-Plasse (left), Jonah Hill (center), and Cera (right) in a scene from Superbad.

depiction of teen anxiety and vulnerability. Reviewer Claudia Puig, writing in *USA Today*, noted that "humiliation, fear, and occasional elation are the dominant emotions for these bumbling but oddly likable young men" and added that audiences would react to the movie with "side-splitting laughter, along with some powerful cringing." *Newsweek* reviewer Devin Gordon deemed Cera and Hill "a duo for the ages" and praised Cera as "a world-class sputterer. He delivers all his lines a split second faster than you expect, turning each joke into a sneak attack."

Debuting in August 2007, *Superbad* was the No. 1 film in the nation during its first two weeks of release and proved to be a summer favorite. Its popularity and high-profile promotion campaign gave Cera a great deal of exposure, including newspaper and magazine profiles and appearances on television talk shows. It was a sign of things to come: just one month after *Superbad* made him a star, his next film project debuted, and it proved to be even more popular.

Juno

Cera's next role was in the 2007 film *Juno*. In winning that role, he had the good fortune to be part of a small-budget independent film that ended up

*Cera with Ellen Page,
his co-star in* Juno.

being one of the most talked about pictures of the year. The title character, played by Ellen Page, is a smart and sharp-tongued 16-year-old who gets pregnant and considers having an abortion before deciding to find someone to adopt the baby. Cera played Paulie Bleeker, the teenage father of the baby, though he and Juno are better described as friends than as lovers, and their relationship manages to survive the difficulties they find themselves in.

The movie drew a lot of attention for dealing with the hot-button topics of teen sex and abortion, but, as several reviewers noted, *Juno* focuses on the experiences of its characters rather than promoting a social message. "*Juno* is not really about the realities of teen pregnancy or of adoption," wrote David Heim in *Christian Century*. "It is a clever riff on teen lingo and a cheerful fantasy of how a sense of humor and a good friend can get you through almost anything." *New Yorker* writer David Denby was another critic who was very positive about the film, proclaiming it "a coming-of-age movie made with idiosyncratic charm and not a single false note." A surprise hit with filmgoers, *Juno* won acclaim at film festivals and then went on to do big business across the nation, racking up more than $143 million in domestic sales after being made for the relatively low sum of $7.5 million. The film received four Academy Award nominations, including consideration as Best Picture, and screenwriter Diablo Cody took home the Oscar for Best Original Screenplay.

Though Cera was not the principal character in *Juno*, he made a big impression. Todd McCarthy, writing in *Variety*, noted that "Cera's low-key modesty and reserve prove an effective counterbalance" to Page's more outgoing character. Similarly, *Maclean's* writer Brian D. Johnson asserted that "Cera, with his skinny legs in jogging shorts and his sincere puppy-dog charm, must be the most laid-back leading man/boy to ever make comedy romantic."

Such comments illustrate Cera's growing reputation as a celebrity heart-throb, despite the fact that he usually plays characters with somewhat "geeky" personalities. He had gotten his first taste of that kind of attention during his promotional work for *Superbad*. During an appearance at Comic Con International in San Diego, for instance, he was fawned over by a succession of young female fans proposing marriage. When questioned about his status as a "hottie," Cera responds with low-key bewilderment. "A sex symbol?" he said in disbelief at a 2008 press conference.

"Like I symbolize sex?" He has also pointed out that he is not a conventionally handsome type. "If you stood me in line with all my ex-girlfriends and asked who's more attractive, it's always them." While typical movie-star perfection may not be his stock in trade, Cera's appeal is widespread, especially among teenage girls, and some observers see him as a new type of leading man. Noting the actor's "sad baby-seal cuteness and mastery of the uncomfortable pause," an *Entertainment Weekly* feature in June 2008 asserted that "Cera has made teenage awkwardness not just funny but cool."

——— **"** ———

"Juno is not really about the realities of teen pregnancy or of adoption," wrote David Heim in **Christian Century.** *"It is a clever riff on teen lingo and a cheerful fantasy of how a sense of humor and a good friend can get you through almost anything."*

——— **"** ———

Nick & Norah's Infinite Playlist

Cera's ability to play a romantic lead was put to a demanding test in *Nick & Nora's Infinite Playlist*, which debuted in October 2008. Once again cast as a high school senior, Cera plays Nick, an aspiring rock musician who falls for Norah, portrayed by Kat Dennings. Their romance is kindled during an evening when they travel through New York City with a small group of fellow teens on a quest to find a secret concert being staged by one of their favorite bands.

While *Nick & Norah's Infinite Playlist* did not repeat the blockbuster success of *Juno*, the film did receive mostly positive reviews. *Chicago Tribune* reviewer Michael Phillips was one of those who gave the film high marks and singled out Cera's perfomance: "The way he acts and reacts, he's especially astute at capturing a certain kind of young adult, perched on a fence between hesitant adolescence and premature middle age." David Ansen, writing in *Newsweek*, declared that "the movie has a genuine, unforced sweetness. Its

*An example of the chemistry between Cera and his co-star,
Kat Dennings, in* Nick & Norah's Infinite Playlist.

charm is in the details, the attitude, the slowly building chemistry between
Cera (a master of stone-faced irony) and the beguiling Dennings."

The rapport between the actors resulted partly from the film's production process. Director Peter Sollett brought the cast together before beginning the filming so that they could get comfortable with one another.
"We all hung out before shooting, so we weren't total strangers," explained Cera. "We played poker, played PS3, watched movies, talked."
There was also a sense of shared adventure once the cameras rolled,
which largely came from the film's shooting locations. "We had some
crazy nights filming the movie," noted Dennings. "Well, you know, middle of the night in New York City, drunk people throwing things, yelling
at us, wanting us out of their places where they like to be." Cera's status
as a rising celebrity also inspired some of the production disruptions,
with vocal onlookers sometimes interrupting scenes by shouting "Hey,
Superbad!" when they caught sight of the actor.

An Uncertain Star

As his fame has grown, Cera has become increasingly unhappy about all
the attention he receives in public. "When you're in a movie that's really
popular, it's a strange life change," he observed. "Literally overnight people

recognize you on the street. Sometimes they're nice, sometimes they're not, and sometimes they lose track of how to treat other human beings." He also finds it difficult to interact with fans who assume they know what he's like because of his on-screen personas. "I'm not like these parts I play, you know. I mean, it's just acting. I do the work on the set, and then it's over."

Despite his misgivings, Cera is likely to receive a lot of attention for upcoming films, which include *The Year One, Youth in Revolt,* and *Scott Pilgrim vs. the World.* Once those projects are completed, he has suggested that he might focus on smaller parts to avoid some of the negative aspects of being a star. "I don't really want to be famous, and I'm kind of scared that might be happening," he admitted. "I guess I need to make sure that it's worth all that comes with it."

HOME AND FAMILY

Cera splits his time between an apartment in Los Angeles and his parents' home in Brampton.

HOBBIES AND OTHER INTERESTS

An amateur musician, Cera formed a band called The Long Goodbye with Clark Duke but doesn't expect that they will devote a lot of time to developing the act. "Now that people know me as an actor, I don't think they'd be able to get past that and listen to the music," he noted. In addition, Cera is said to be composing music for the upcoming film *Paper Hearts,* and he also writes short stories in his spare time.

SELECTED CREDITS

Television Programs

"Rolie Polie Olie," 1998 (voice of animated character)
"I Was a Sixth Grade Alien!," 1999-2001
What Katy Did, 1999 (TV movie)
Custody of the Heart, 2000 (TV movie)
My Louisiana Sky, 2001 (TV movie)
"The Grubbs," 2002
"The Berenstain Bears," 2003 (voice of animated character)
"Arrested Development," 2003-2006

Films

Steal This Movie, 2000
Frequency, 2000

Confessions of a Dangerous Mind, 2002
Superbad, 2007
Juno, 2007
Nick & Norah's Infinite Playlist, 2008

Internet Series

"Clark and Michael," 2006

HONORS AND AWARDS

Beaver Award (Canadian Comedy Foundation for Excellence): 2008, Best Film Actor, for *Superbad*

FURTHER READING

Periodicals

Entertainment Weekly, Aug. 17, 2007, p.20; Oct. 17, 2008, p.76
Globe and Mail, Oct. 3, 2008
Los Angeles Times, Sep. 7, 2008
New York, Aug. 6, 2007
New York Times, July 8, 2007; Sep. 28, 2008, p.11
Newsweek, Sep. 27, 2008
Times (United Kingdom), Oct. 4, 2008
USA Today, Aug. 17, 2007, p.D8

ADDRESS

Michael Cera
Thruline Entertainment
9250 Wilshire Blvd., Ground Floor
Beverly Hills, CA 90212

Michael Cera
Paradigm Talent Agency
360 North Crescent Drive, North Building
Beverly Hills, CA 90210

WORLD WIDE WEB SITES

http://www.clarkandmichael.com
http://www.sonypictures.com/homevideo/superbad
http://www.foxsearchlight.com/juno
http://www.sonypictures.com/movies/nickandnorah

Heidi Klum 1973-

German Supermodel
Host of the Hit Reality TV Show "Project Runway"

BIRTH

Heidi Klum (pronounced *kloom*) was born on June 1, 1973, in Bergisch Gladbach, Germany. Bergisch Gladbach is a small city located east of the Rhine River, about six miles from the larger city of Cologne. Klum's father, Gunther, worked as an executive at a cosmetics and perfume company, and her mother, Erna, was a hairdresser. Heidi has one older brother.

YOUTH

As a young girl growing up in Bergisch Gladbach, Klum's life was fairly ordinary. "I had a very normal childhood with my brother and my parents, who are still together," she recalled. "We were always very close and would talk to each other about what we did during the day." Klum took ballet and jazz dance classes and developed an interest in fashion design. She liked to spend time shopping and hanging out with her friends. Her memories of childhood include favorite foods, such as her mother's sauerkraut soup, her grandmother's potato dumplings, and sweets, especially black licorice and hazelnut ice cream.

——— ———

"My father was always early out of the house and coming home late," Klum recalled. "I saw that in order to make money—we didn't have a lot, but we did do things like go on holiday [vacation]—I understood it was because my father worked so hard."

——— 〟 ———

Both of her parents worked, and Klum learned at a young age the value of working hard for what she wanted. "My father was always early out of the house and coming home late," she recalled. "I saw that in order to make money—we didn't have a lot, but we did do things like go on holiday [vacation]—I understood it was because my father worked so hard."

EDUCATION

Klum attended Integrierte Gesamtschule Paffrath (IGP) in Bergisch Gladbach. IGP is a German public school roughly equivalent to a U.S. middle and high school, where students are prepared to go on to a university. Art and math were her favorite subjects in school. Klum completed her studies in June 1992 and planned to enroll in a university in Dusseldorf, Germany, to study fashion design.

CAREER HIGHLIGHTS

Becoming a Model

Klum was interested in becoming a fashion designer and wanted to learn about the business side of the fashion industry. She never considered a career as a model until one day in the winter of 1991, when she happened to see a magazine ad for the Model 92 nationwide modeling contest in Germany. The contest was sponsored by *Petra* magazine and a New York mod-

Hair and make-up are a constant part of a model's work preparation.

eling agency. The winner would appear on national television in Germany and receive a $300,000 cash prize along with a three-year modeling contract. When her best friend Karin suggested that she enter the contest, Klum laughed at the idea.

But Karin continued to encourage Klum to enter, finally convincing her to send the application. Klum posed for a few photos wearing a bikini and mailed in her contest entry. Five months later, in the spring of 1992, she learned that she had been chosen for the final round of the competition. She went on to win the contest, beating 30,000 other contestants for the title of Model 92.

Abandoning her university plans, Klum used her contest prize winnings to begin modeling professionally when she was 19 years old. She knew that the choice to try modeling was a risk, but she was willing to take the chance. Klum started out with small jobs in Hamburg and Berlin, Germany, posing for a knitting magazine and modeling for women's clothing catalogs. She soon wanted more exciting modeling jobs and decided to leave Germany for the high-profile fashion runways of Paris, France and Milan, Italy.

Overcoming Rejection

During the early 1990s when Klum was beginning her modeling career, it was fashionable for runway models to be extremely thin and unsmiling. The most successful runway supermodels of that time, such as Kate Moss, were known as waifs. The word originally meant a child who was undernourished, frail, and homeless or lost. When used to describe a fashion model, a waif was an uncommonly thin woman who looked like a sad child. With her curvy figure and brilliant smile, Klum did not fit this image at all.

In Paris and Milan, Klum heard that she was too healthy-looking, too wholesome, and that her overall appearance was too American. She had a hard time finding work as a model. "In the beginning.... I was being rejected all the time. When I started, Kate Moss was the hottest thing. It was not about being proud and upright with the smile glowing—a powerful woman. It was more about being a crushed, crumbled person in the corner, the beaten-down girl looking a little sad and tired."

In spite of this obstacle that seemed impossible to overcome, Klum was committed to building a career in modeling. She refused to give up. If she couldn't be a model in a runway fashion show, she was determined to find another kind of modeling work. "There were still other things out there for people who were normal-looking. You don't always have to go through the front door to get what you want.... When I figured out that editorial [magazine photos] and runway weren't really my thing because I am voluptuous and not this stick that you had to be at that time, I just found other ways to be a model."

Klum used her determination and self-confidence to push through the nearly constant rejection. Fashion designer Michael Kors told *In Style* magazine, "Fashion goes back and forth between the healthy bombshells and the waifs, and she came in to see me in Paris in the 90s during a sad-waif moment. In walked Heidi with glorious teeth and curves, and she was like, 'I know I'm not what's in right now, but I had to meet you.' That confidence struck me immediately."

Eventually, though, Klum became frustrated with the limited opportunities for her in the European fashion world. She asked her agency to transfer her to the U.S., and in the summer of 1993 she moved to Miami, Florida. After just a few months there, she moved again—this time to New York City.

In New York, Klum shared a rundown apartment with two other struggling German models. At first, adjusting to life in the U.S. while trying to land modeling jobs was extremely stressful. One of the other girls gave up and returned to Germany. Klum, however, was more determined than ever to succeed. "I was more ambitious, more business savvy. When everyone went out drinking, I went home.... You can't wait for things to come to you, especially in this business."

Klum went on hundreds of casting calls and was hired for many small jobs. Her first big success was appearing on the cover of *Self* magazine. During this time, most of her work still involved modeling for such catalogs as Newport News, Chadwick's, and J.C. Penney. While other models made catalogs their entire career, Klum never gave up her belief that there were bigger opportunities for her.

Breaking Through

Over the objections of her booking agent, Klum insisted on getting an appointment with the prestigious lingerie designer Victoria's Secret. Klum recalled, "My booker said I wasn't good enough and I said, 'It's great that you think that, but I want them to tell me that.'" Her confidence carried her through that first meeting, and in the end the Victoria's Secret executives

Klum's appearance on the cover of Sports Illustrated *magazine, shown here, was the big break she'd been working for.*

loved her. Klum walked in her first Victoria's Secret runway show in 1997. She soon became one of the most recognizable Victoria's Secret Angels, and one of company's top models.

This success lead to new opportunities for Klum, such as appearances on television talk shows, which in turn opened more doors for her. As a guest on a 1997 episode of "Late Night with David Letterman," she surprised everyone with her yodeling talent. An editor at *Sports Illustrated* magazine saw the show and thought that her charm would be a good fit for the magazine's swimsuit edition. Although Klum was not as well-known or as experienced as the models that *Sports Illustrated* usually hired, she landed the cover of the 1998 swimsuit edition. She later said of this milestone breakthrough, "Before that, no one connected my name with my face. From that day on, people could."

Klum soon became one of the fashion industry's highest-paid models. Her photos appeared on the covers of many major fashion magazines in the U.S. and Europe, including *Vogue*, *Marie Claire*, *Elle*, *GQ*, *Glamour*, and

Mademoiselle. As an established supermodel, Klum decided to use her growing celebrity status to branch out into acting. Appearing in movies and television shows seemed like a natural progression for her career.

In 1998, Klum made her acting debut with a recurring role in the television comedy series "Spin City." Appearances on many television shows in both the U.S. and Germany followed, with Klum acting for some roles and playing other parts as herself. In 2001, Klum's roles included an appearance on the popular cable television drama "Sex and the City" and a small part in the movie *Zoolander*. She appeared in guest roles in several TV series, was a guest on various television and radio talk shows, and was frequently seen in special programs about modeling and fashion.

"Project Runway"

In 2002, Klum was invited to collaborate on the development of a new reality television show called "Project Runway," envisioned as a competition for aspiring fashion designers. Klum was interested in the idea, but reluctant to participate at first. "I didn't think I was that good on camera," she later explained. She also wasn't sure of the level of involvement she would have if she became the host of "Project Runway." She said, "I didn't want to just show up and do the normal things I do when I am modeling." Klum decided to join the show once she was assured that she would be able to influence its direction. "I wanted to have some input into the show and have some ideas brought in. I liked the aspect of being more than just the host."

The "Project Runway" season begins with 16 contestants who are ready to compete. At the start of each episode, Klum and others present a design challenge to test the competitors' skills, creativity, and ability to perform under pressure. The designers are often asked to create high-style garments out of unusual materials or within unexpected restrictions. Some of the challenges have required the use of such odd materials as recycled items, edible foods, car parts, Hershey wrappers, apartment furnishings, plants and flowers, and other materials not traditionally used in clothing. Other challenges have involved designing for celebrities, including Tiki Barber, Victoria Beckham, Apolo Anton Ohno, Sarah Jessica Parker, Brooke Shields, and their own mothers. Still others have required creating a certain type of garment, like a prom dress, a wedding dress, a letter carrier uniform, or an outfit for a professional wrestler.

The contestants listen to the challenge, sketch some ideas, choose fabric and trim, sew the garments, select accessories, fit the models, and oversee the models' hair and makeup. They spend much of their time in the

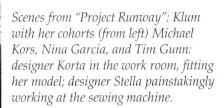

Scenes from "Project Runway": Klum with her cohorts (from left) Michael Kors, Nina Garcia, and Tim Gunn: designer Korta in the work room, fitting her model; designer Stella painstakingly working at the sewing machine.

work room, with frequent visits from mentor Tim Gunn, formerly the chair of fashion design at Parsons The New School for Design and now Chief Creative Officer at Liz Claiborne. At the end of each episode, the designers mount a runway show with their creations, and a team of judges—including Klum, fashion designer Michael Kors, and fashion magazine editor Nina Garcia—judge their work and select a contestant to eliminate. The final few contestants have a chance to show their designs during the prestigious New York Fashion Week. The ultimate winner receives a cash award, a chance to start his or her own fashion line, and other prizes.

In addition to showcasing the work of new designers, each episode also features the squabbles, arguments, catty comments, personal dramas, and conflicting personalities of the competitors. Almost from the beginning, fans discussed and debated each episode's challenges, the judges' comments, contestants' behavior, the quality of work, and elimination decisions on Internet blogs and forums. Klum has admitted to being surprised by the show's success, saying, "I thought that people would like 'Project Runway,' but I didn't think they would get so obsessed!"

> **"**
>
> *Klum was reluctant to join "Project Runway" until she was assured that she would be able to influence its direction. "I didn't want to just show up and do the normal things I do when I am modeling," she explained. "I wanted to have some input into the show and have some ideas brought in. I liked the aspect of being more than just the host."*
>
> **"**

Perhaps Klum's most well-known contribution to "Project Runway" is her signature send-off for each week's eliminated contestant. She explained how the German phrase "auf Wiedersehen" was chosen for this purpose. "We were filming the first show and still didn't have the line to say goodbye to people. We were brainstorming, people were shouting, nothing was working, and then I got it.… I came up with it because it means 'I'll see you again.' It's meant to be a nice way to say goodbye, and it's not mean because that's just not who I am."

"Project Runway" debuted on the Bravo cable network in December 2004, and the show was an immediate success. It became one of Bravo's most popular shows in its first year, with more than two million viewers each week. Quickly gaining a cult-like following, the show was praised by both fans and critics as a standout reality TV series. The success of "Project

Runway" was attributed to its outrageous design challenges, and it also gained credibility with a process for judging and eliminating contestants that was seen as fair and sensible. The first five seasons of "Project Runway" were each nominated for at least one Emmy award. In 2008, Klum received an Emmy nomination for Outstanding Host for a Reality or Reality-Competition Program.

Klum has mentioned several episodes as some of her most favorite moments. Her favorite designer challenge was the very first one, when contestants were given $50 to buy materials from a grocery store to make their garments. "That set the tone [for the competition] and that showed people out there, 'Wow, they think beyond the garbage bag.'" Another of her favorite challenges was in the second season, when the designers had to make new garments using only the clothes they were wearing at that moment.

A Full Career

Along with her duties as host and executive producer of "Project Runway," Klum finds time to work on many other projects. Her television appearances have included an episode of the popular crime drama "CSI: Miami" (2003) and the comedy series "How I Met Your Mother" (2007). Klum also had a part in the movie *Ella Enchanted* (2004), and a brief appearance as herself in *The Devil Wears Prada* (2006). In 2004, she published *Heidi Klum's Body of Knowledge: 8 Rules of Model Behavior*, a book that she describes as being "about trying different things and not being afraid of getting pushed back sometimes. It's about being creative to get ahead." In 2006, Klum created the reality television show "Germany's Next Topmodel," a competition based on "America's Next Top Model" which she hosts and produces for German television.

Klum continues to model in runway shows and magazines, primarily for Victoria's Secret, and has expanded her business ventures to include her own collections of perfume, swimsuits, Jordache jeans, Birkenstock sandals, fat-free candy, jewelry, skin care products, and more. Klum is very particular about endorsements and insists on being involved in product development. She said, "I need to have complete control over how something is going to look if my name is going to be attached to it."

Although she works hard to maintain control over her public image, Klum has a more relaxed attitude about her physical appearance. "I don't want to be wondering about how skinny I am, wondering what I'm going to eat because I don't want to gain and I want to look hot and young, always and forever…. You see so many people going out for plastic surgery…. I'm not

Klum works the runway in this Victoria's Secret fashion show.

going to do that. I want to get older and I'm going to have wrinkles. Beauty comes from the inside.... I drink lots of water and sleep! For me, sleep is holy, otherwise I don't feel fit and I don't look as good."

MARRIAGE AND FAMILY

Klum married stylist Ric Pipino on September 6, 1997. They divorced in 2003. Klum and singer Seal (Sealhenry Samuel) were married on May 10, 2005, in Costa Careyes, Mexico. Seal and Klum first met in the lobby of the Mercer Hotel in New York City when a mutual friend introduced them. At the time, Klum was five weeks pregnant with her first child, conceived with ex-boyfriend Flavio Briatore, an Italian Formula One racing executive. "I was not looking for anybody," Klum later confided. "[Seal] was just there. He walked in the door.... He looked good. I was like, 'Wow.'"

The couple were engaged one year later. Seal proposed to Klum on top of a glacier in the Canadian Rockies. "He took me by helicopter. He had an igloo built there ... rose petals, candies. Very, very romantic! There was food and champagne, and then the helicopter left. It was a little scary, too, because you're so cut off from the world. No trees, nothing.... But I was ecstatic. I loved it. It was wonderful."

Klum has three children. Her daughter with Briatore, Leni, was born in 2004, followed by her two children with Seal, Henry (born in 2005) and Johan (born in 2006). The family divides their time between homes in Los Angeles, California, Costa Careyes, Mexico, New York City, and Bergisch Gladbach, Germany.

> " *"I don't want to be wondering about how skinny I am, wondering what I'm going to eat because I don't want to gain and I want to look hot and young, always and forever.... You see so many people going out for plastic surgery.... I'm not going to do that. I want to get older and I'm going to have wrinkles. Beauty comes from the inside."* "

Reflecting on the challenges of balancing her celebrity status, her career, and family, Klum said, "I have a normal life and I have this glamorous life, but to me it's two different things. It's not like I'm this glamour diva who hands everything over and I just sit on my throne at home. When we're at home, we're cooking and doing things with the kids, driving them to school. We do the things that everyone has to do.... I never thought I would walk down the street and be followed by paprazzi, married to Seal, who I listened to when I was still in Germany. I never dreamed of this life because I didn't know there was a life like this."

HOBBIES AND OTHER INTERESTS

Klum enjoys spending time with her family and friends, playing tennis, ballet and jazz dancing, traveling, skiing, snowboarding, going to flea markets, and painting. She remains close to her parents and visits Germany often. She is also affiliated with charitable organizations, including the American Red Cross and the Elizabeth Glazer Pediatric AIDS Foundation.

SELECTED CREDITS

Writing

Heidi Klum's Body of Knowledge: 8 Rules of Model Behavior (To Help You Take Off on the Runway of Life), 2004

Television Appearances

"Spin City," 1998-99
"Project Runway," 2004- (creator and host)

Movie Appearances

Blow Dry, 2001
Ella Enchanted, 2004
The Life and Death of Peter Sellers, 2004

HONORS AND AWARDS

50 Most Beautiful People (*People* magazine): 2001
Style Icon of the Year (*Us* magazine): 2008

FURTHER READING

Periodicals

Entertainment Weekly, July 11, 2008, p.36
Forbes, June 30, 2008, p.96
Harper's Bazaar, May 2006, p.204
In Style, June 2006, p.274
Marie Claire, June 2008, p.78
People, May 14, 2001, p.140; Dec. 13, 2004, p.54; Mar. 28, 3005, p.73; May 9, 2005, p.156; July 24, 2006, p.102
Redbook, Feb. 2005, p.90; July 2008, p.112

Us, Apr. 28, 2008, p.66
USA Today, Dec. 3, 2007, p.D3

Online Articles

http://www.bravotv.com/Project_Runway/bio/heidi_and_tim/Heidi_Klum
(Bravo, "Heidi Klum: Bio," 2007)

ADDRESS

Heidi Klum
"Project Runway"
Bravo
3000 West Alameda Ave., Suite 250
Burbank, CA 91523

WORLD WIDE WEB SITES

http://www.heidiklum.com
http://www.bravotv.com/project-runway

Courtesy, Deutsche Grammophon

Lang Lang 1982-

Chinese Classical Pianist
First Chinese Performer Nominated for a Grammy
Award

BIRTH

Lang Lang (pronounced *Long Long*) was born June 14, 1982, in Shenyang, a large industrial city in western China. His mother, Zhou Xiulan, worked as a telephone operator. His father, Lang Guoren, was a police officer. Lang Lang is their only child.

YOUTH

Lang Lang's parents wanted him to be a pianist even before he was born. Their own dreams of careers in the performing arts ended during China's Cultural Revolution (1966-1976), a period in Chinese history known for repression and persecution by the government. Chairman Mao Zedong led a political campaign to revolutionize Chinese society. In the process, thousands of people were killed and millions were imprisoned or exiled. Cultural works that criticized Mao or his policies were forbidden, and many artists, musicians, and intellectuals were forced to give up their work and to do manual labor instead.

Before that point, Lang Lang's father played the erhu, an ancient stringed instrument sometimes called the Chinese violin. He had been the concert-master (primary violinist and assistant to the orchestra's conductor) for a traditional Chinese orchestra in Shenyang. His mother had enjoyed singing and dancing and had hoped to become a concert singer. After the Cultural Revolution ended and people were once again free to study the arts, Lang Lang's parents became determined that their child would achieve the goals that they had been forced to abandon.

When Lang Lang's mother was pregnant with him, she listened to classical music as much as she could, hoping that her baby would be born with a love of music. When Lang Lang was just a year old, his father started teaching him the musical scale. Lang Lang could read music before he could read letters or words. Every day, a local radio station played two hours of classical music by such European composers as Ludwig von Beethoven, Johannes Brahms, Frederic Chopin, and many others. Lang Lang's parents played this music for him when he was a baby, hoping to encourage his interest in it. When he was about two years old, his parents bought him an old upright piano that cost about half of the money they earned in one year. The piano took up most of one room in their small apartment.

Beginning to Play Piano

As a young child, Lang Lang liked to watch cartoons on television. When he was about three years old, he saw a "Tom and Jerry" cartoon in which Tom the cat played the piano while being teased and tormented by Jerry the mouse. The piano music happened to be a piece by the famous Hungarian composer Franz Liszt, and Lang Lang later described this as his first memorable exposure to western classical music. Seeing this cartoon motivated Lang Lang to learn how to play the piano himself. Lang Lang said, "'Tom and Jerry,' of all things, opened my eyes. I thought, 'I want to be like that cat!'" Lang Lang immediately began taking piano lessons and soon proved to be a musical prodigy—a child with exceptional talent.

Lang Lang's father expected his young son to become the best pianist in China. Even at age three or four, Lang Lang was expected to practice his piano lessons for several hours each day. One day, his father was angry at him for playing games instead of practicing the piano, and he threw all of Lang Lang's favorite transformer toys out the window. When Lang Lang ran outside, he found that most of his toys had broken when they fell from the apartment window. As an adult, he was able to be philosophical about the pressure placed on him at such a young age. "Once you become a pianist, you need to give up part of your childhood," he acknowledged. "I was always jealous of other people when they would go to the park and I would be practicing."

> "
>
> *"Once you become a pianist, you need to give up part of your childhood," Lang Lang acknowledged. "I was always jealous of other people when they would go to the park and I would be practicing."*
>
> "

In 1987, when Lang Lang was five years old, he gave his first public recital in the Shenyang Piano Competition. The contest was for piano students under the age of ten. "Right away, I really liked to perform.... Even then I wanted to be a world-class pianist. The piano felt very connected to me, and giving recitals, I felt totally relaxed, no nerves at all. I loved being on stage." Lang Lang won the competition, beating nearly 500 other young piano students.

EDUCATION

When he was seven years old, Lang Lang enrolled in the Shenyang Conservatory of Music, where he continued to study piano in addition to the usual school subjects. His favorite classes were literature, history, and geography. Meanwhile, his father created a schedule for Lang Lang that included a minimum of six hours of piano practice at home each day.

By the time Lang Lang was eight years old, his talent as a pianist had developed so much that he could learn nothing more from his teachers in Shenyang. To continue developing his talent, Lang Lang would have to find more experienced teachers. "Shenyang was a nice place to begin study, but not a good place to develop," he recalled. "My parents decided I should go to a more cultured place: Beijing. I could see a lot of great pianists play there, ... attend master classes with some of them, and also hear better orchestras and good conductors." His parents made the difficult decision to have Lang Lang study in Beijing, with the goal of being accepted to the Beijing Central Music Conservatory.

In his autobiography Playing with Flying Keys,
Lang Lang describes some of the challenges he faced while growing up.

Leaving Home

In 1991, when Lang Lang was eight years old, he and his father moved to Beijing. His mother stayed behind in Shenyang, keeping her job there and sending money to support her husband and young son. Shenyang was a 12-hour train ride from Beijing, which meant that Lang Lang would not be able to see his mother very often. The decision was hard on the family. His mother later said, "At the time, Lang Lang was very small. It was very hard to say goodbye to him. I can never forget. His mouth was quivering, and then he and I both started up. He cried and I cried. But for his work, for the piano that he loves so much, I let him go."

In Beijing, Lang Lang and his father lived together in a tiny one-room apartment. It was only 100 square feet in size—the piano took up most of the space in the apartment. Also, it had no heat and no bathroom. The apartment building provided just one bathroom for each floor, and Lang Lang and his father shared the bathroom with three other families. The Beijing winters were long, cold, and damp, and Lang Lang often wore all of the clothes he owned, all at once, to try to stay warm. The apartment building was also infested with mice, and he would often wake up in the morning to find his music books chewed to pieces. His father worried that mice would bite Lang Lang's hands, preventing him from playing the piano.

To prepare for his audition with the Beijing Central Music Conservatory, Lang Lang practiced for many hours each day, much to the annoyance of his new neighbors. The apartment walls were thin, and neighbors would bang on the walls or shout to complain when he played the piano too late at night. His father insisted that Lang Lang practice until 11:00 at night and start again very early in the morning. Finally, the neighbors called the police, who negotiated a compromise on the number of hours that Lang Lang would play the piano.

Beijing was a much larger, busier, and more populated city than Shenyang. Lang Lang attended school and continued piano lessons, but he had no friends. His northern Chinese accent branded him as an outsider and made it difficult to communicate with people in Beijing. His intense schedule of piano practice and schoolwork left him with almost no time for himself. Lang Lang struggled with loneliness and missed his mother terribly.

Despite his dedication to practicing, even Lang Lang's piano lessons were going badly. His new teacher was mean, and she eventually dismissed Lang Lang as her student. This was the worst possible thing that could have happened. "It was a very difficult time. I was trying hard, but my lessons were going badly, and just before I was supposed to audition for the top music school in the country, the Central Conservatory, my teacher kicked me out of her studio. She told me that I wasn't meant to be a pianist, and that was devastating."

Quitting—and Starting Again

Lang Lang's father became enraged, convinced that his son's failure had shamed the family. He went so far as to demand that eight-year-old Lang Lang kill himself in shame. Horrified by his father's words, Lang Lang instead decided to stop playing the piano. Even after his father apologized and begged Lang Lang to begin playing again, he refused. He didn't speak to his father or touch a piano for four months.

Finally, Lang Lang's anger at his father faded and he did start playing the piano again. "At my school, the music teacher asked me why I wasn't playing anymore. I started crying and said, 'My teacher told me that I had no talent.' The schoolteacher put this Mozart sonata on the piano and said, 'Come on, play the slow movement.' So I did, and as I performed I suddenly realized how much I loved the instrument. Playing … brought me hope again."

Lang Lang began studying with a new teacher and resumed preparations for his audition with the Beijing Central Conservatory. Of the 3,000 students who would audition for a place in the Conservatory's fifth grade, only 12 would be accepted. The pressure was the most intense he had ever experienced. Lang Lang wrote about the experience in his autobiography, *Playing with Flying Keys*, recalling how nervous he had been waiting in the audition line for half the day. When his turn finally came, he recalled, "As I adjusted the piano bench and positioned my fingers on the keys, however, a great calm washed over me…. My mind cleared. I began to play and nothing distracted me." After two rounds of auditions, Lang Lang was ranked number one.

When he was nine years old, Lang Lang began studying at the Beijing Central Music Conservatory. There he played on a grand piano for the first time. "For so many years, I had only played on upright pianos. The grand piano was like a new world. A whole new world of sound!" Lang Lang's focus on being the number one pianist in China intensified and soon expanded to include the goal of being number one in the world. He began entering as many competitions as he could.

A Winning Streak

Lang Lang's emphasis on competitions was soon rewarded. In 1993, he won first prize at the Fifth Xing Hai Cup Piano Competition in Beijing. In

Lang Lang at the piano. © Photo: J. Henry Fair/Deutsche Grammophon.

1994, when he was 12 years old, Lang Lang took first prize and a special award for outstanding artistic performance at the Fourth International Young Pianists Competition in Germany. Lang Lang then went on to win the 1995 Tchaikovsky International Young Pianists Competition in Japan.

Later in 1995, Lang Lang performed Chopin's "24 Etudes" at the Beijing Concert Hall. The "24 Etudes" are difficult, complicated, and challenging pieces for even the most skilled pianists. In the classical music world, the successful performance of the "24 Etudes" demonstrates a complete mastery of the piano. Lang Lang performed the "24 Etudes" to great critical acclaim when he was only 13 years old. This success led to his 1996 appearance as a soloist in the first concert of the China National Symphony.

Leaving China

By the mid-1990s, Lang Lang was receiving invitations to study at music conservatories all over the world. After sending a video of one of his concert performances, he was invited to audition in person for enrollment in the prestigious Curtis Institute of Music in Philadelphia, Pennsylvania. After two rounds of auditions, he was granted admission to the Curtis Institute, which included full tuition, housing, meals, and living expenses. In 1997, when Lang Lang was 15 years old, he and his father moved from China to live in Philadelphia.

In his autobiography, Lang Lang wrote in detail about how difficult it was to leave his mother again and move to the United States, a world away from his home in China. But he knew it was a necessary move if he was to develop his talent any further. "Western classical music in China is usually like Chinese food in the West—familiar but not quite the real thing," he observed. "A lot of musicians here [in China] don't do much beyond play the notes themselves.... The sound is nice enough, but there is none of that intensity. That is what I had to come to the West to learn."

Lang Lang and his father were given a large apartment to live in, which was very different from their home in Beijing. Most notably, this apartment had heat and its own bathroom. Lang Lang was amazed by all the new privileges he had. The Curtis Institute provided him with a Steinway grand piano in his apartment. The school also hired a private tutor to teach him English.

Lang Lang was also surprised when his new American piano teacher told him that he would not be entering any more competitions. In China, that had been the way for music students to advance their careers. But in the U.S., Lang Lang was instructed to focus on achieving his own personal best. His teachers told him to focus on his own work, and not to compare himself to others. When he was ready, they said, the right opportunity would come.

CAREER HIGHLIGHTS

A Big Break

Lang Lang's first big professional opportunity came in 1999 when he was 17 years old. He was called as a last-minute substitute soloist for a concert with the Chicago Symphony Orchestra at the Ravinia Music Festival. The scheduled pianist had fallen ill and was unable to perform. Lang Lang said, "Before this concert, one day my friend and I were in a bookstore and saw an ad for Ravinia. I said to my friend, if I play in this kind of concert, I will be world famous."

The performance was a great success. The *Chicago Tribune* called Lang Lang the "biggest, most exciting keyboard talent encountered in many years." For his part, Lang Lang said, "I wasn't actually nervous … but it was so exciting and so surprising. This was my first time playing with such a world-famous symphony, especially in a gala concert." Lang Lang later told the *New Yorker* that he imagined Michael Jordan's slam dunk as he struck his first resounding chords and Tiger Woods's golf swing while he played the octaves. After the concert, world-famous vi-

HAYDN
SONATA IN E MAJOR
RACHMANINOFF
SONATA NO. 2
IN B-FLAT MINOR
BRAHMS
SIX PIECES, OP. 118
TCHAIKOVSKY
DUMKA
NOCTURNE IN C-SHARP MINOR
BALAKIREV
ISLAMEY

RECORDED LIVE AT SEIJI OZAWA HALL, TANGLEWOOD

Lang Lang released his first recording, which included two live concerts at Tanglewood, when he was just 19.

olinist Isaac Stern invited Lang Lang to play a private recital for the musicians.

After this debut, Lang Lang was invited to perform concerts all over the world. He decided to combine his studies at the Curtis Institute with concert tours. During 2001, he toured Europe, performed at the prestigious Carnegie Hall in New York City, and returned to China for the first time in four years as part of a tour with the Phildelphia Orchestra. Lang Lang also released his first recording in 2001, *Haydn, Rachmaninoff, Brahms, Tchaikovsky, Balarkievy,* which included two concerts he performed in Tanglewood, Massachusetts. In 2002, Lang Lang completed his formal studies at the Curtis Institute and became an official

Steinway artist, agreeing to perform exclusively on pianos made by Steinway & Sons.

Lang Lang's early professional performances were a success with audiences but received mixed reviews from critics. One writer for the *New York Times* said, "Virtuoso fireworks are only a part of the story; and rather than being merely flashy, they reveal a deep underlying power." The *Chicago Tribune* praised his first recording for "stupendous pianism" and the "seemingly effortless way he has of enlisting the piano's full resources to realize the music beyond the printed page." However, a writer for the *American Record Guide* called Lang Lang's playing "superficially impressive" and "exhausting to listen to."

> "I practice now much more in my head than at the piano. The best thing to do is close your eyes and visualize the score of what you're working on. You can do a lot of work that way, deciding on the direction of a phrase, the articulation, and other things.... Music without that kind of attention is nothing. If you play without it, you're getting some of the feeling, but you don't really understand what the piece is about."

Life on the Road

Since 2002, Lang Lang has spent most of his time touring, giving concerts and teaching master classes all over the world. He averages 125 performances each year. "I love the audience because I love the tension there ... because it seems like a lot of people watching, I mean, the creation of this wonderful work. And then you are at the same time the interpreter. It's like building a bridge to their heart."

Even with such a grueling travel and performance schedule, Lang Lang still manages to practice at least four or five hours a day. But his piano practice now is very different from when he was a young boy. "I practice now much more in my head than at the piano. The best thing to do is close your eyes and visualize the score of what you're working on. You can do a lot of work that way, deciding on the direction of a phrase, the articulation, and other things. So by the time you get to the piano, you've already made a lot of progress.... I spend a lot of my practice time going over the score, noticing where the harmony changes, where the orchestration shifts, and so on. So when I begin to practice the piano part, I've already done a lot of work on the piece.... So music without that kind of attention is nothing. If you play without it, you're getting some of the feeling, but you don't really understand what the piece is about. That's what practice time is for; it's to reach an understanding of the piece."

Lang Lang also uses his time away from the piano to study the history, literature, and culture of the historical period in which music was composed. "You must do a lot of research to connect the music with its time, and to our own," he observed. "Reading literature of the time helps you to understand what people were thinking during that time. So when you play a piece, you understand its entire history better, and when you play, it's more real to you. When you read a book, it tells you what's going on. But when you play music, it becomes real life.... Every time I play, I try to see the images. For example, I see something. I can see [a] beautiful forest and everything's green."

Inspiring Young People

Lang Lang's phenomenal success at such a young age has inspired a generation of young musicians around the world. In China, the "Lang Lang Effect" refers to the growing number of children studying piano because of Lang Lang. His popularity with children resulted in the creation of five "Lang Lang Steinway" pianos, designed especially for early music education. In 2004, he became an International Goodwill Ambassador to the United Nations Children's Fund (UNICEF). In this role, Lang Lang raises awareness of the needs and rights of children throughout the world. "Music is like a language, it's like a universal language, it has the connection to the people and also the feeling from your soul, from your heart. I think the best way to reach children is to play them music, this really opens their ears and their minds." In 2008, the Lang Lang International Music Foundation was created to further inspire and educate young musicians.

Lang Lang has been featured on countless television programs and in newspapers and magazines around the world. A documentary film, *Dragon Songs* (2006), follows him on a concert tour of China. In addition, he has been invited to perform for events broadcast around the world, including the opening ceremony of the 2008 Summer Olympics in Beijing. There Lang Lang performed for a stadium audience of 90,000 and billions of television viewers worldwide. In 2008, he became the first Chinese performer to be nominated for a Grammy Award, for Best Instrumental Soloist Performance with Orchestra. He is also the first classical artist ever to perform an exclusive concert in the digital world of the "Second Life" video game.

*Lang Lang played with five-year-old Li Muzi
at the opening ceremonies of the 2008 Olympics in Beijing.*

Also in 2008, Lang Lang published his autobiography, *Journey of a Thousand Miles: My Story*, along with a version for young readers titled *Playing with Flying Keys*. In these books, he describes the life of dedication that led to his success as a pianist, including details about the stress and pressure placed on him by his strict and demanding father. Readers may be surprised by the trials and difficulties that young Lang Lang endured under his father's high expectations. *Booklist* called his story "suspenseful and engrossing." *Kirkus Reviews* praised the book as "a true rags-to-riches story told with fervor and variety," while *Children's Bookwatch* called it a "dynamic, moving story."

HOME AND FAMILY

When he is not touring, Lang Lang divides his time between homes in New York City and Beijing. He lives and travels with his father. Although his mother's primary home is in China, she often also travels with Lang Lang.

At his solo concerts, Lang Lang often invites his father to perform encores with him. For these encores, he and his father play traditional Chinese compositions. "I want to continue my family tradition, that we love playing together and performing for people," he commented. "Secondly, I love to promote Chinese culture and its musical instruments. Thirdly, my father was the principal for the erhu section in an excellent Chinese orchestra. He sacrificed his own career that he didn't play for ten years for my sake. Being able to perform in major concert halls in the world must have been in his dream. It is the least that I could do to help him fulfill that dream."

HOBBIES AND OTHER INTERESTS

Lang Lang is an avid fan of NBA basketball. His favorite team is the Philadelphia 76ers, and he also follows the career of Chinese basketball star Yao Ming. Lang Lang still enjoys watching cartoons when he can, along with movies and sports, including soccer and ping-pong. He is fascinated with any kind of technology gadget. Lang Lang admires professional golfer Tiger Woods and has said that Woods is a role model for living with fame and running the business of being a performer. Lang Lang is also a fan of jazz and hip-hop music. His favorite pop artists include Christina Aguilera, Beyoncé, and Alicia Keys.

SELECTED RECORDINGS

Hadyn, Rachmaninoff, Brahms, Tchaikovsky, Balarkirev, 2001
Rachmaninoff: Piano Concerto No. 3, Scriabin Etudes, 2002
Tchaikovsky, Mendelssohn: First Piano Concertos, 2003
The Banquet Soundtrack, 2006
Dragon Songs, 2006
Memory, 2006
Beethoven Piano Concertos 1+4, 2007
The Painted Veil Soundtrack, 2007

HONORS AND AWARDS

Leonard Bernstein Award (Schleswig-Holstein Music Festival): 2002
President's Merit Award (Recording Academy): 2007

FURTHER READING

Books

Lang Lang, and Michael French. *Lang Lang: Playing with Flying Keys,* 2008
Lang Lang, and David Ritz. *Journey of a Thousand Miles: My Story,* 2008

Periodicals

American Music Teacher, Mar. 2008, p.22
Baltimore Sun, Apr. 15, 2001, p.9

Christian Science Monitor, Feb. 7, 2008, p.1
Current Biography Yearbook, 2003
Keyboard, Nov. 1, 2003, p.32
New York Times, Sep. 2, 2003, p.E1
New Yorker, Apr. 2, 2007, p.86; Aug. 4, 2008, p.52
People, Sep. 29, 2003, p.42; Nov. 19, 2008
Time, Nov. 17, 2001, p.137
U.S. News & World Report, June 11, 2001, p.66
Washington Post, Apr. 15, 2001, p.G1

Online Articles

http://www.cbsnews.com/stories/2005/01/07/60minutes/main665508.shtml
    (CBS News: 60 Minutes, "Lang Lang: Piano Prodigy," Jan. 9, 2005)
http://www2.deutschegrammophon.com/artist/biography?ART_ID=LA
    NLA
    (Deutsche Grammophon Gesellschaft, "Lang Lang Biography," June
    2008)
http://www.people.com/people/package/gallery/0,,20237714_20241212_20
    545183,00.html
    (People, "2008's Sexiest Men Alive: Lang Lang," Nov. 19, 2008)
http://www.unicef.org/people/people_lang_lang.html
    (UNICEF, "UNICEF People: Lang Lang," undated)

ADDRESS

Lang Lang
Lang Lang International Music Foundation
146 West 57th Street, Suite 36D
New York, NY 10019

WORLD WIDE WEB SITES

http://www.langlang.com
http://www.thelanglangfoundation.org

Leona Lewis 1985-

British Singer
Performer of the Hit Songs "Bleeding Love" and
"Better in Time"

BIRTH

Leona Louise Lewis was born on April 3, 1985, in the Isling-
ton section of north London, England. She is of mixed ances-
try, with a Guyanese father and a mother of Welsh, Italian, and
Irish descent. Her father, Joe Lewis, is a youth corrections officer and a former DJ, and her mother, Maria Lewis, is a social
worker who has also taught ballet. Leona has two siblings—a
younger brother, Kyle, and an older half-brother, Bradley.

YOUTH AND EDUCATION

Lewis had a working-class upbringing. When she was five years old her family moved to Hackney, a multicultural neighborhood in East London. She has warm memories of those years and the support she received from her parents, who eagerly fostered her natural gifts. Her talent and passion were obvious from the beginning. "I remember singing into my hairbrush," Lewis recalled, "and every chance I could I'd be doing a show or performing in the front room for my family."

> "I remember singing into my hairbrush," Lewis recalled, "and every chance I could I'd be doing a show or performing in the front room for my family."

When Lewis was six, she attended the Sylvia Young Theatre School to learn about singing and acting. The school fees were high, and her parents had to work multiple jobs to make ends meet. When Lewis was nine she advanced to the prestigious Italia Conti Academy and also began private voice lessons. By this point, however, the school fees became unaffordable and she had to transfer to a local public school. For the next two years she struggled to enjoy herself, complaining that the new school stifled her creativity.

Another door opened for Lewis when she was accepted at the BRIT School of Performing Arts and Technology, a renowned state-funded institution. For the next three years, she studied piano and guitars and soaked up knowledge about the entertainment field. She also began regularly hanging out with performers and musicians. Additional information about Lewis's school years is unavailable, and it's unclear whether she graduated or left school before finishing her degree.

FIRST JOBS

Near the end of her time at the BRIT School, Lewis began seeking out a recording contract. A demo that she recorded when she was 15 years old secured her an audition with Sony Records, although the label declined to sign her. For several more years she persistently promoted herself by recording more demos and sending them to labels. Booking studio time was expensive, however, so she worked a series of part-time jobs: as a cashier at the Gap, a waitress at Pizza Hut, and a receptionist for a mortgage adviser.

Lewis with Ray Quinn, another finalist from "The X Factor."

Lewis also found work as a performer, playing gigs at clubs in London. In addition, when she was 18 she secured a part in *The Lion King* musical at Disneyland in Paris, France. The idea of living that far from home did not appeal to her, however, so she turned down the job.

CAREER HIGHLIGHTS

"The X Factor"

After so many years of studying music and performing without a record deal, Lewis was discouraged. At one point, she considered putting her dreams on hold to go to college and pursue a career in social work. But in 2006, her boyfriend persuaded her to audition for "The X Factor." The British television series pits singers against each other in a closely followed competition. The winner usually receives a recording contract negotiated by Simon Cowell, the show's creator and one of its judges/mentors.

Lewis passed the audition and proceeded to stun the judges as well as millions of viewers each week. Her extensive vocal range was on full display with her renditions of such popular standards as "All By Myself," "Over the Rainbow" (in the style of one of her favorite singers, Eva Cassidy), and "I Will Always Love You," made popular by another of her idols, Whitney

Houston. Lewis advanced to the finals, which aired live on December 6, 2006, and attracted 13 million viewers. With a stellar performance of "A Moment Like This," Lewis clinched the title, winning a record deal worth 1 million pounds (roughly $1.5 million).

Along with winning the prize, Lewis received a serious endorsement from the finale's guest judge, Gary Barlow of the popular vocal group Take That. "This girl is probably 50 times better than any other contestant you have ever had," Barlow told Cowell, "so you have a big responsibility to make the right record with her." As a judge, Cowell is notoriously difficult to impress, but he agreed with Barlow, proclaiming Lewis "one of the best singers we've had in this country for 20 years."

While her popularity was still high after her victory on "The X Factor," Lewis released a studio recording of "A Moment Like This" a few weeks later on Cowell's BMG label. The single set a Guinness World Record for single-week sales by tallying 50,000 downloads in 30 minutes.

Launching a Singing Career

Cowell and Lewis were careful about the next big step. They decided to assemble a whole team of industry experts. High on their list of collaborators was legendary music executive and producer Clive Davis, credited with discovering Whitney Houston and helping to launch the careers of Alicia Keys and Kelly Clarkson. (For more information on these performers, see the following issues of *Biography Today*: for Houston, see *Biography Today*, Sep. 1994; for Clarkson, see *Biography Today*, Jan. 2003; for Keys, see *Biography Today,* Jan. 2007.)

Cowell knew how to spark Davis's interest. "You might have the next Whitney Houston on your hands," he told the CEO. Assured of Lewis's potential, Davis began a plan to break her into the U.S. market. He scheduled a showcase for her in February 2007 at the Hilton Hotel in Los Angeles, where Lewis performed before a room full of record label executives and songwriters. Not long after, Davis and Cowell collaborated to form a joint label, J Records/Syco Music, that would feature her as its first artist. Lewis signed a five-album contract worth $9.7 million.

Lewis and the record company executives soon assembled a superstar squad of producers and songwriters, including Akon, Ne-Yo, Dallas Austin, and Max Martin. As Lewis went to work on her CD, she wanted to ensure that her debut was a serious artistic statement and that it accurately represented her. "I wanted to make an album that was totally me," she said. "Each song is about something that either I've gone through or that someone around me has gone through." As a result of her deliberate pace, along with a bout of tonsillitis that briefly sidelined her voice, the highly anticipated album took several months to record. Fans began wondering if the album would ever be released.

In November 2007, Lewis's debut finally reached the record stores. *Spirit* was released in the United Kingdom, with an American version scheduled for a later release. The album features "Bleeding Love," a catchy, soulful number with a heavy R&B beat, as well as ballads, cover songs, and two tracks that Lewis co-wrote, "Here I Am" and "Whatever It Takes."

Record sales proved that *Spirit* was worth the wait. "Bleeding Love" was that year's biggest-selling week-one single, moving over 200,000 copies in just seven days. The album performed even better, selling over 375,000 copies in its first week, which made it the United Kingdom's fastest-selling debut album of all time. Although the album was not yet released in the United States, critics couldn't help noticing the buzz *Spirit* had caused. "Lately she's been earning justified comparisons to Celine Dion, Whitney Houston, and yes, Mariah Carey," reported Nicholas Fonseca in *Entertainment Weekly*. "So divas, watch out." (For more information on Dion, see *Biography Today*, Sep. 1997; for more information on Carey, see *Biography Today*, Apr. 1996.)

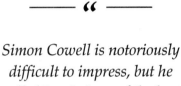

Simon Cowell is notoriously difficult to impress, but he called Lewis "one of the best singers we've had in this country for 20 years."

Breaking Out in the U.S.

Team Leona Lewis pulled no punches when it began promoting the U.S. version of *Spirit*. By spring 2008, she had been featured on the cover of *Harper's Bazaar UK*, and *Entertainment Weekly* had listed her among the "8 to Watch in 2008."

Davis scheduled Lewis to sing at his pre-Grammy Awards party, which according to some reports is a bigger celebration than the Grammys. After giving a stirring performance of "Burning Love," she had the pleasure of mixing with the stars in attendance, many of whom were her childhood idols. "I nearly spontaneously combusted because everyone on my iPod was there!" she exclaimed. "Carrie Underwood, Alicia Keys, and I met Whitney Houston—that was crazy."

Lewis's debut CD, Spirit, *was a big success in the UK and in the U.S.*

The U.S. version of "Bleeding Love" hit stores on March 18, 2008. A day before its release, Lewis appeared with Oprah Winfrey on her popular daytime talk show. Lewis's performance of "Bleeding Love" received a standing ovation. In the days leading up to the release of *Spirit* on April 8, she endured an exhausting string of photo shoots, interviews, and performances. Grabbing the most attention were her appearances on "Good Morning America," "The Tonight Show with Jay Leno," and "Jimmy Kimmel Live!"

As in Great Britain, *Spirit* made a big splash in the U.S. market. It took the top spot on the *Billboard* album chart, selling 205,000 copies. The "Bleeding Love" single sold even better. Lewis became the first British female solo artist to scale the top of the Hot 100 singles chart in more than 21 years.

"Bleeding Love" eventually became iTunes' top-selling single of the year. Her second single, "Better in Time," also reached the *Billboard* Pop 100 chart, peaking at the No. 4 spot.

The critical reaction to *Spirit* was also positive. Writing in *Essence*, Kiera Mayo said that "Leona Lewis is a stunning vocal powerhouse" and has "the pitch and range of Mariah Carey, topped with the powerful pop appeal of Christina Aguilera." In the magazine *Interview*, Matt Diehl wrote, "Lewis's strength is her powerful voice: as showstopping as Whitney Houston's, as wrenchingly human as that of Lewis's favorite, Eva Cassidy."

In the wake of her accomplishments in the first half of 2008, Lewis received special honors during the rest of the year. In June she was invited to perform in London at the 90th birthday celebration of Nelson Mandela, a Nobel Peace Prize winner and the first black South African president. She also had the rare opportunity of rocking out with Jimmy Page, the legendary guitarist of Led Zeppelin, at the closing ceremonies of the 2008 Summer Olympics in Beijing, China. In December 2008, she was asked to join Beyoncé, Jay-Z, and other stars to commemorate the inauguration of U.S. president Barack Obama in January.

—— " ——

While singing at a pre-Grammy Awards party, Lewis had the pleasure of mixing with the stars in attendance, many of whom were her childhood idols. "I nearly spontaneously combusted because everyone on my iPod was there!" she exclaimed. "Carrie Underwood, Alicia Keys, and I met Whitney Houston— that was crazy."

—— " ——

Future Plans

With a promise of a long career before her, Lewis said she no plans to stop producing music. She told *Glamour* magazine in October 2008 that she was thinking about beefing up her style by doing "rockier stuff." She also began to explore acting opportunities.

HOME AND FAMILY

Lewis maintains strong ties to her old neighborhood and her family. She still lives near her parents and her brothers in the Hackney section of London. She and her boyfriend, Lou Al-Chamaa, have been friends since

childhood—they met when she was 10 years old, and they lived on the same street. When she's home she likes spending time with Al-Chamaa and another family member, a rottweiler named Rome.

MAJOR INFLUENCES

As a child growing up in the 1990s, Lewis enjoyed listening to pop music and R&B. There were several female divas who first inspired her to sing, including Whitney Houston, Christina Aguilera, and Eve Cassidy. By listening to the records her dad spun as a DJ, she also grew familiar with stars from past generations, artists like Stevie Wonder, Michael Jackson, and Minnie Riperton, a soul singer who like Lewis was known for her multi-octave voice.

HOBBIES AND OTHER INTERESTS

Away from the spotlight, Lewis's life is low-key. Occasionally, she will spend a night dancing in clubs, but she has no interest in hard partying (to her, alcohol "tastes like hairspray"). A night at home relaxing with friends or having a nice meal is just as appealing for her. To stay fit, she swims and rides horses, a hobby that she learned from her mother.

Lewis's passion for social causes has led her to participate in various fundraisers. She recorded the ballad "Footprints in the Sand" to help support the organization Sport Relief, which also coordinated her February 2008 trip to South Africa. She also joined 14 other female singers to record "Just Stand Up," a song that was released in September 2008 to benefit Stand Up to Cancer, an organization that raises funds for cancer research. That same month, the vocal group performed the song live during the Stand Up to Cancer telethon, which aired on major networks all over the world.

Lewis is also an animal activist and a vegan (someone who doesn't eat meat or use any products derived from animals). She announced in 2008 that she wants to develop an apparel line that promotes the humane treatment of animals. "I would love to promote an affordable line of non-leather bags and shoes," she said. "I'm trying to find the right companies to work with, sourcing different things and talking to creative teams."

SELECTED CREDITS

Television

"The X Factor," 2006

Recordings

Spirit, 2006 (UK release); 2007 (U.S. release)

HONORS AND AWARDS

MTV Asia Awards: 2008, Breakthrough Artist
World Music Awards: 2008, Best Pop Female and Best New Act

FURTHER READING

Periodicals

Billboard, Oct. 6, 2007; Dec. 1, 2007; Jan. 26, 2008; July 19, 2008; Aug. 16, 2008
Daily Telegraph, Oct. 18, 2007
Entertainment Weekly, Nov. 30, 2007; Dec. 14, 2007; Apr. 11, 2008; July 25, 2008
Glamour, Oct. 2008
Houston Chronicle, Apr. 20, 2008
Independent, Mar. 28, 2008
Interview, Mar. 2008
Observer, Dec. 17, 2006; Mar. 30, 2008
People Weekly, Apr. 28, 2008
Sunday Mail, Oct. 21, 2007
Times (London), Dec. 18, 2006; Nov. 15, 2007; Mar. 8, 2008; Mar. 27, 2008; Oct. 18, 2008; Nov. 1, 2008
US Weekly, Apr. 7, 2008

Online Articles

http://www.thisislondon.co.uk
(Evening Standard, "X Factor SuperStar: Leona Lewis on Fame, Fear of Failure and the Pressures of Being Simon Cowell's Biggest Hope," Oct. 21, 2007; "British Idol Leona Lewis Tops the U.S. Charts … But Still Can't Afford to Buy a House in London," Mar. 27, 2008)
http://www.rollingstone.com
(Rolling Stone, "Leona Lewis: British R&B Diva Wins Over Simon Cowell," Apr. 3, 2008)
http://www.seventeen.com
(Seventeen, "Fun Stuff, When I was 17: Leona Lewis," May 5, 2008)

ADDRESS

Leona Lewis
J Records
1540 Broadway, Suite 9W
New York, NY 10036

WORLD WIDE WEB SITES

http://www.leonalewismusic.co.uk
http://www.jrecords.com
http://www.xfactor.itv.com

Jef Mallett 1962-

American Cartoonist
Creator of the Comic Strip "Frazz"

BIRTH

Jeffrey Alan Mallett was born on February 28, 1962, in Howell, Michigan. His parents are Gordon Mallett, a retired music teacher, and Janet Mallett, a violinist and church organist who performs for various orchestras. A middle child, Jef has an older sister, Martha, and two younger siblings, Sarah and Edward.

Mallett created "Birchbark," his first comic strip, during high school.

YOUTH

Mallett was three years old when his family moved across Michigan to Big Rapids, a small city in the west-central region of the state. Not long after settling into his new home, Mallett showed an early interest in cartoons. By reading comics he learned how to read, as well as how to draw.

By the time Mallett turned 10 he had become determined to create comic art. He wrote to the National Cartoonists Society and requested a brochure that described how to be a cartoonist. As he continued to follow the comics and teach himself techniques, he soon learned that being a cartoonist demanded the skills of a good storyteller as well as a good artist. "I thought, 'Well, I'd better learn to write,'" he remembered, "and by god that was fun too, I really loved writing."

Mallett soon took advantage of opportunities to present his cartoons to others, distributing his comic strips around school and publishing them in his church's bulletin. He increasingly became more comfortable with promoting himself and his cartoons. (Already drawn to the limelight, he had earlier dropped the second "f" from his first name so that it stood out a bit more.)

A break came in high school, when he was paid $5 a week to write a daily comic strip for *The Pioneer*, the newspaper in Big Rapids. The strip, a series called "Birchbark," followed a French-Canadian adventurer and his Native American guide and ran for two to three years. Looking back, Mallett considered doing "Birchbark" a good introduction to the world of comics.

EDUCATION

Mallett graduated from Big Rapids High School in 1980. He decided to remain near home and enroll in Ferris State College (now known as Ferris State University) to receive training as a paramedic. After a year, he decided to shift his focus and transferred to Butterworth Hospital School of Nursing in Grand Rapids. Around that time, he also joined the staff of the local newspaper, the *Grand Rapids Press*, as a writer and illustrator. Confident that he could support himself working for a paper, he decided he did not need a fallback career and dropped out of nursing school.

Becoming a Cartoonist

A span of 20 years bridged the publication of "Birchbark" and the debut of "Frazz," the comic strip that put Jef Mallett on the map. In a biographical comment on the National Cartoonist Society web site, he states that he "got distracted" during those two decades. That may be the case, but his newspaper years were still productive ones. He worked at the *Grand Rapids Press* from 1981 to 1987 as a writer and illustrator. In 1987 he moved to the *Flint Journal* and added "columnist" to his list of responsibilities. Two years later, he moved to Lansing, Michigan, the state capital, to work for the Booth Newspapers' central branch. There he served as art director and editorial cartoonist.

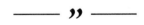

When Mallett started creating comic strips, he soon learned that being a cartoonist demanded the skills of a good storyteller as well as a good artist. "I thought, 'Well, I'd better learn to write,'" he remembered, "and by god that was fun too, I really loved writing."

In his new job, Mallett was assigned a number of positions: art director, graphic artist, photo editor, editorial cartoonist, and copy editor. Composing editorial cartoons—illustrations with a political and social message—was rewarding for Mallett, who had always enjoyed discussing philosophy and ideas. Also, as a copy editor—someone who ensures that newspaper articles read well and are free of grammatical errors—he could further sharpen his writing skills. He remembers his experiences in Lansing fondly. "It was actually really great because it was a small office, so you learned to do a little bit of everything," he said.

CAREER HIGHLIGHTS

Launching Out on His Own

By 1996, Mallett was publishing a couple of editorial cartoons a week for Booth Newspapers. That year he also introduced himself to a new audi-

Frazz enjoying a moment with students.
FRAZZ: © Jef Mallett/Dist. by United Feature Syndicate, Inc.

ence by publishing an illustrated children's book titled *Dangerous Dan*. The story followed a mischievous young daydreamer whose creativity cannot be contained. With his imagination, little Dan transforms his notebook into a flying carpet and his backyard into a jungle.

Mallett promoted *Dangerous Dan* by touring elementary schools, reading his book at student assemblies. The readings proved to be a great opportunity. Not only did Mallett get to interact with children, but he also stumbled upon an idea for a new character. During the assemblies, Mallett couldn't help noticing that the huge task of calming down students for his presentation often fell to the school janitor, who succeeded because he had a special connection with the students. "That's when I noticed that the janitor was 'the man,'" Mallett said. "He's the guy that all the kids looked up to." The idea for a popular elementary school custodian named Edwin Frazier ("Frazz") was born.

Mallett began working out the essential details of Frazz and his world. From the onset, he decided that Frazz was the kind of guy who liked his job, even though janitorial work is unglamorous and even though he has other career options. Frazz is also a songwriter who penned a few hit songs that continue to pay him royalties. "He likes it," Mallett explained of Frazz's situation. "He's not there because he has to be."

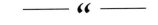

According to Mallett, "Basically, I just try and make [Frazz] me, only me if I was a lot cooler than I am."

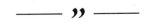

Along with deciding that Frazz is content as an elementary school janitor, Mallett gave his character other passions to round out his personality. It is no coincidence Frazz's interests—literature, philosophy, cycling, running—are also Mallett's. It was a matter of the artist following the conventional wisdom of "write what you know." According to Mallett, "Basically, I just try and make him me, only me if I was a lot cooler than I am."

Frazz Discovers Friends—and Readers

Mallett's imagination continued to fill out the details of Frazz's world at Bryson Elementary. More characters took form and began interacting with the janitor, and a few became regulars. There is Mr. Burke, Frazz's best friend, an engaging teacher who often riffs with the janitor about big concepts while they play one-on-one basketball or cruise the bike trails. There is also Caulfield, a bright and clever third-grader named after Holden Caulfield of *The Catcher in the Rye*, who talks with Frazz to relieve his boredom. Caulfield's antics often land him in detention with his teacher, the stern Mrs. Olsen. (The punishment is bearable because it at least gives the third grader the opportunity to discuss books with Frazz.) Another major character is Miss Plainwell, the attractive first-grade teacher who has caught Frazz's eye.

In April 2001, Mallett landed a deal with United Feature Syndicate, a large company that sells comics to newspapers throughout the country and the world. He began producing daily strips while keeping his job with Booth

FRAZZ: © Jef Mallett/Dist. by United Feature Syndicate, Inc.

Newspapers. "I played it safe (in terms of security, if not health and sanity)," Mallett joked.

After a year juggling the daily strip and his newspaper job, Mallett resigned from his full-time position. By that time, "Frazz" had been introduced to 50 newspapers, which is not a huge number compared to established strips, which through syndicates can reach as many as 2,000 newspapers. Nonetheless, "Frazz" had backing from many believers, including Meegan Holland, Lansing bureau chief for Booth Newspapers. "Jef is one of those few people who can translate a concept into a few clever words and fun pictures," she told the *Lansing State Journal*. Like Holland, fans appreciated the subtle humorous style that became the strip's defining trait.

Readers immediately took note that in the world of "Frazz," kids like Caulfield and his peers expressed plenty of insight. Mallett has said that their maturity was a central part of his original vision. "There's an assumption that kids are somehow inferior to adults, and that's just plain wrong," he remarked. "They leave adults in the dust when it comes to figuring things out."

Young readers were not the only ones affected by the comic's strip fresh perspective on kids. Gene Weingarten, a *Washington Post* columnist and a friend of Mallett's, had a similar reaction. "It's the best cartoon I've ever seen at living in two worlds at the same time," he said to the *Lansing State Journal*. "It absolutely appeals to kids and it absolutely appeals to adults. His characters are existing in a kids' milieu, but it does not patronize kids who are reading it."

Expanding into a Major Market

As Mallett worked to introduce "Frazz" to more newspapers, it helped that the strip had fans in the newspaper business. Friends like Weingarten did

FRAZZ: © Jef Mallett/Dist. by United Feature Syndicate, Inc.

their part to help promote the comic strip and expand its audience. By 2005, the *Washington Post* had added "Frazz" to its comics page, as had other major papers like the *Chicago Tribune* and the *Los Angeles Times*. In total, 150 newspapers were carrying Mallett's strip.

Of course, Mallett was happy for more readers to find his work. It was more gratifying to learn that people were not only reading "Frazz" but also talking about its heady ideas. Another *Washington Post* columnist, Michael Cavna, began writing about the strips. He devoted some of the entries on his blog, "Comic Riffs," to exploring various concepts and cultural references in Mallett's strips. That type of response was not a surprise for Mallett, since he believed attentive readers like Cavna were out there. "You don't get dumb people reading the newspapers. You get the smarter people, the college graduates, the movers and shakers," he said.

Some readers also appreciated the values that Mallett promoted through his characters, as well as the racial and cultural diversity of Bryson Elementary. In 2003, the Religion Communicators Council bestowed him the Wilbur Award for "excellence in the communication of religious values." More recognition came in 2004 from the National Cartoonists Society, which listed "Frazz" as a finalist in the Best Comic Strip of the Year category. The following year, Mallett received the Wilbur Award again.

"Frazz" had earned a place among other nationally read comics, and so in 2005 Mallett published the first collection of cartoons, *Live from Bryson Elementary*. Over the next three years, two more collections were published: *99% Perspiration* (2006) and *Frazz 3.1416* (2008). The books' titles were examples once again of the clever allusions Mallett's readers had come to expect: "99% Perspiration" refers to a quote by Thomas Edison ("Genius is 1% inspiration and 99% perspiration") and the numbers "3.1416" are the first five digits of pi (the famous numerical ratio used in math).

Comic strip collections offer Mallett's fans more opportunities to enjoy the strip.

Other Works

Regularly cranking out editorial cartoons and comic strips can be demanding, but Mallett still has been able to take on other projects as an illustrator. During his early newspaper days, he developed a working relationship with *Detroit Free News* columnist Mitch Albom, best known for his best-selling memoir *Tuesdays with Morrie*. Mallett illustrated two of the columnist's collected writings—*Live Albom II* (1990) and *Live Albom IV* (1995). Over the years, Mallett has also been a regular guest on the nationally syndicated morning radio program "The Bob and Tom Show" and has been recruited twice to do cover art for that duo's sketch comedy albums.

Mallett has also found work that directly related to his two favorite hobbies, cycling and competing in triathlons (endurance races that combine swimming, cycling, and running). He illustrated *Roadie: The Misunderstood World of a Bike Racer* (2008) by Jamie Smith, an insider's guide on the life of the cyclist fanatic. Other steady gigs that Mallett has landed for sports periodicals include writing a column for *Inside Triathlon* magazine and publishing one-panel cartoons for the bicycle racing periodical *VeloNews*.

After illustrating a book on cycling, it seemed fitting that Mallett would embark on a guide about triathlons as well. Drawing from his training as a journalist, Mallett decided to take on the dual role of writer/illustrator. With a working title of *Trizophrenia: Inside the Minds of a Triathlete*, the book is scheduled to be released in fall 2009 by Velo Press, which also published *Roadie*. *Trizophrenia* is "about the way triathletes train, think, and live," said Mallett. "It's sort of like *Roadie* and yet very different."

MARRIAGE AND FAMILY

Mallett lives his wife, Patty, in a modest ranch home in Lansing. They have been married since 1988. She plays a pivotal role in the production of "Frazz" as the official "letterer," the person who draws the comic strip's text. As a professional communications manager, Patty has the right skills for crafting the strip's dialogue. Jef has been vocal about his gratitude for his wife's contribution to "Frazz." "[Her] normal handwriting is better than just about anybody's careful lettering.... [She is] one of the best copy editor/proofreaders I know," he said.

Luckily for Jef, Patty enjoys cycling as well. He calls riding tandem with her his "top cycling priority." Both also work together to help stray pets at the Capital Area Humane Society.

MAJOR INFLUENCES

Frazz the janitor exhibits much in common with the Calvin of the legendary strip "Calvin and Hobbes," even though Frazz is a few decades older. Both characters regularly discuss philosophy and use difficult words that often send readers reaching for their dictionaries. In fact, the similarities between the two were so striking for some comic strip followers that they helped fan rumors that the true creator of "Frazz" was not Jef Mallett, but "Calvin and Hobbes" creator Bill Watterson. Internet chatter helped spread the rumors about the strip's false authorship. Mallett, who considers Watterson a huge influence, has made an effort to put the rumor to rest, declaring he is not Watterson, nor is he trying to replace "Calvin and

Cycling and triathlons are Mallett's two favorite sports—and Frazz's, as well.
FRAZZ: © Jef Mallett/Dist. by United Feature Syndicate, Inc.

Hobbes" with his cartoon. "You might as well try to replace or copy the Mona Lisa," Mallett said in praise of the older strip.

Along with modeling his work on elements of established strips like "Calvin and Hobbes," Mallett looks for inspiration from great storytellers, like 20th-century novelist John Steinbeck and contemporary novelist Richard Russo. He also has said that he learns a lot reading humor writer Bill Bryson and considers him among his favorites. As a mark of his respect, Mallett even named the elementary school in "Frazz" after Bryson.

HOBBIES AND OTHER INTERESTS

Mallett's pursuits outside of work are by no means ordinary. Among his former pastimes, he has flown hang gliders and airplanes. In recent years, however, he has focused more on competing in cycling races and triathlons. He has been running competitively since he was a teenager, and he has also been a cycling aficionado for nearly just as long. By adding swimming to that repertoire, he entered the world of Olympic-distance triathlons (competitions that involve swimming 0.9 miles, cycling 25 miles, and running 6.2 miles).

Of his two favorite sports—cycling and triathlon—Mallett devotes more attention to triathlons since the balanced nature of the sport does not demand cycling very long distances, which he says can be dangerous. Being in top physical condition, which is essential for competing in triathlons, has a practical value for Mallett: "I'm not as efficient with the job or the family if I'm not in shape." Along with the physical benefits, Mallett enjoys the bragging rights of frequently taking first place in his age group.

Impressed by Mallett's fitness record, in 2006 television producers of the reality adventure show "Nevada Passage" invited him to compete on a two-person team against 18 other athletes. The one-hour feature show, which is syndicated on national networks, stages outdoor competitions like cycling and auto racing in various locales throughout the country. Mallett and his teammate, a freelance writer from New York, did not win the competition, but they had the distinction of appearing on a show that draws 2 million annual viewers.

As if completing a regular triathlon wasn't a great enough feat, in November 2008 Mallett reached his long-held dream of finishing the ultimate endurance test, the Ironman triathlon (a longer race that involves a 2.4-mile swim, a 112-mile bike, and a 26.2-mile run). He loved the experience and looks forward to participating in more Ironmans in the years ahead.

SELECTED WRITINGS

"Frazz"

Frazz: Live from Bryson Elementary, 2005
99 Percent Perspiration, 2006
Frazz 3.1416, 2008

Other Works

Live Albom II, 1990 (by Mitch Albom, illustrated by Mallett)
Live Albom IV, 1995 (by Mitch Albom, illustrated by Mallett)
Dangerous Dan, 1996
Roadie: The Misunderstood World of a Bike Racer, 2008 (by Jamie Smith, illustrated by Jef Mallett)

HONORS AND AWARDS

Wilbur Award (Religion Communicators Council): 2003, 2005, Editorial Cartoons/Comics category
Best Comic Strip of the Year Finalist (National Cartoonists Society): 2004, for "Frazz"

FURTHER READING

Periodicals

Albany Times Union, Mar. 3, 2004
Grand Rapids Press, May 9, 2006
Lansing State Journal, May 12, 2004; Jan. 27, 2005; Dec. 18, 2007
News & Observer, Nov. 24, 2006
San Antonio Express-News, Oct. 11, 2008

Online Articles

http://www.capitalgainsmedia.com
   (*Capitalgains,* "The Frazz with Jef Mallett, Cartooning Genius," Jan. 16, 2008)
http://www.ncs-glc.com/GLC/jef_mallett/jefmallett.html
   The GLyph, "'… The janitor was always the coolest guy …': A Chat with Jef Mallett," Apr. 7, 2005)
http://www.suite101.com
   (*Suite101.com,* "2003 NEA Holiday Comics Special, by Jef Mallett, Creator of Frazz," Dec. 23, 2003)
http://www.velonews.com
   (*VeloNews,* "Author Jamie Smith and Illustrator Jef Mallett Launch Book at Kinetic Systems," Apr. 1, 2008; "Q&A: Cartoonist Jef Mallett on 'Frazz,'" May 23, 2004)
http://voices.washingtonpost.com
   (*Washingtonpost.com,* "The Morning Line:'Frazz' & the Evolution of a Comic Mystery," Aug. 8, 2008)

ADDRESS

Jef Mallett
United Feature Syndicate
200 Madison Avenue
New York, NY 10016

WORLD WIDE WEB SITES

http://www.comics.com/comics/frazz
http://www.unitedfeatures.com

Warith Deen Mohammed 1933-2008
American Religious Leader
Former Head of the Nation of Islam and the
American Society of Muslims

BIRTH

Warith Deen Mohammed was born on October 30, 1933, in
Hamtramck, Michigan, the son of religious leader Elijah
Poole Muhammad and Clara Evans Muhammad. His birth
name was Wallace Delaney Muhammad, but in 1978 he
adopted different first and middle names and an altered
spelling of his last name. In addition, he is sometimes re-
ferred to as W. Deen Mohammed and W. D. Mohammed. He

Mohammed was greatly influenced by his father, Elijah Muhammad.

was the seventh of eight children, with older siblings named Emmanuel, Ethel, Lottie, Nathaniel, Herbert, and Elijah, Jr., and a younger brother named Akbar.

YOUTH

Mohammed's childhood—and, indeed, his entire life—was strongly influenced by his father's work in building the Nation of Islam, an African-American religious group. An understanding of Elijah Muhammad and of the movement that he led is essential to understanding the events and ideas that would shape his son.

Originally known as Elijah Poole, the elder Muhammad had grown up in Georgia and later settled in Detroit with his wife, Clara, and their growing family. In 1930, he became a devotee of charismatic leader Wallace Dodd Fard and Fard's newly formed Nation of Islam religious sect. By the time Warith Deen Mohammed was born in 1933, his father had adopted the name Elijah Muhammad and had become the group's chief minister. Fard, who was also known as W. D. Farad Muhammad, mysteriously disappeared in 1934, and Elijah Muhammad claimed leadership of the movement. Soon after, he moved his family to Chicago, where a second Nation of Islam group had been established.

Expanding on the ideas of Fard, Elijah Muhammad refined the religious principles that became the basis of the Nation of Islam, some of which are very controversial. Appealing exclusively to blacks, the group maintains that African Americans are the original and chosen people of Allah (God) while whites are an inferior race of "devils" that was created by a black scientist 6,000 years ago. Rather than seeking peaceful coexistence between the races, the Nation of Islam has been a proponent of black separatism— the idea that African Americans should form their own separate nation. In addition, the group has proclaimed that whites will one day be vanquished by Allah, and blacks will be liberated from oppression. In terms of theology, the religion proclaims that Fard was Allah in human form and that Elijah Muhammad was his divine messenger.

The Nation of Islam's name and some of its practices are derived from the traditional Islamic faith, but there are also important differences between the two groups. Most importantly, followers of traditional Islam do not proclaim superiority for any race. They believe that the prophet Muhammad founded Islam in the seventh century and was the final prophet of Allah. Therefore, the Nation of Islam tenet that Elijah Muhammad is a divine messenger is unacceptable to traditional Muslims. Though the members of the Nation of Islam sometimes refer to themselves as "Black Muslims," followers of mainstream Islam generally do not recognize them as being part of the Muslim faith.

A Turbulent Childhood

Warith Mohammed, who was then going by the name of Wallace, grew up amid the turmoil and the threats that surrounded his father. After Elijah Muhammad took over the Nation of Islam in 1934, he faced harassment from law enforcement agencies, but his most serious opposition came from other followers of Fard, who disputed his leadership. Internal struggles marked by violence continued to be part of the Nation of Islam for decades, and Elijah Muhammad came to rely on a militaristic security force known as the Fruit of Islam to help maintain his hold on power.

Mohammed began to have doubts about his father's religious message when he was still a child. "I had common sense," he later explained, "and my common sense told me this was ridiculous, the idea that God is a God that wants one people to dominate others."

In the mid-1930s, Elijah Muhammad feared that his life was in danger and chose to depart Chicago, leaving his wife and children behind. He spent the next seven years living in other U.S. cities, and during World War II, he served three years in prison for evading the draft—mandatory service in the U.S. military. During this period, Warith Mohammed saw his father only on rare occasions, and he came to view the religious leader as an all-powerful figure whom he both respected and feared.

Warith and his siblings were primarily raised by their mother, Clara, and grew up as part of the Nation of Islam community in Chicago. But even as a young child, Warith Mohammed was no ordinary member of the Nation: he was considered the "chosen son." It was said that Wallace Dodd Fard had predicted that Elijah Muhammad's seventh child would become a great leader. From the time of his birth, Warith, the seventh born, was looked to as the eventual successor to his father, and his special status was indicated by his birth name, Wallace—after Wallace Fard.

EDUCATION

Mohammed attended a school operated by the Nation of Islam in Chicago. In addition, his father wanted him to learn about the traditional Muslim faith, so he attended religious schools taught by Islamic immigrants, and he learned Arabic with a tutor. The language studies allowed him to read the Koran (also spelled Qu'ran), the religious scripture of Islam, in the language in which it was originally composed, and this proved to be an important turning point in his life. He found nothing in the Koran to support the racially based beliefs being promoted by the Nation of Islam. By age 12, he was beginning to have doubts about his father's religious message. "I had common sense," he later explained, "and my common sense told me this was ridiculous, the idea that God is a God that wants one people to dominate others."

Despite his growing skepticism, Mohammed remained deeply involved in the movement, and he joined with other young people in the Junior Fruit of Islam youth group, an experience that he later recalled as one of the happiest of his childhood. Mohammed also undertook studies in some non-religious institutions as an adult. He enrolled in college classes at Woodrow Wilson Junior College and Loop College in Chicago but did not attain a degree. According to some sources, he also studied at the University of El-Azhar in Cairo, Egypt.

CAREER HIGHLIGHTS

By the time Warith Mohammed reached his late teenage years, the Nation of Islam was emerging from its early struggles. Elijah Muhammad had consolidated his power, and the group's membership was growing steadily. The Nation enjoyed its strongest support in poor urban neighborhoods, and its appeal was related to the difficult conditions that existed there. Leaders of the movement made a point of reaching out to those who had struggled with poverty, criminal activity, substance abuse, and other problems. The religion's message of black empowerment and self-affirmation was a welcome sign of hope for many of these individuals, and the Nation's strict code of behavior offered a means of ordering their lives. Members agreed to abstain from tobacco, alcohol, and drugs, to follow specific moral guidelines, and to adopt a modest, neatly groomed appearance. Economic issues also played a part in the group's appeal. The Nation promoted the creation of black-owned businesses and launched several enterprises of its own, including the *Muhammad Speaks* newspa-

A meeting of the Nation of Islam in the early 1960s in Olympia Stadium, Detroit.

per that became prominent in black communities across the country. These ventures ultimately brought great wealth to Elijah Muhammad and members of his family and inner circle.

When he was around the age of 17, Warith Mohammed began preaching in Nation's places of worship, which are known as temples or mosques. At this point, he still supported the movement his father had built, though the influence of the traditional Islamic concepts he had learned in his studies was already evident. In his first sermon, he complained that "we give more attention to the Devil than to Allah," suggesting that the congregation should put more emphasis on their own faith rather than the racial injustices they may have experienced. In some ways, Mohammed seemed ill suited to his role as a religious leader. A shy person who spoke with a lisp, he had little of the fiery charisma and eloquent speech possessed by many preachers, but he balanced these shortcomings with his deep spiritual knowledge and quiet intensity.

After serving as a minister in the Chicago temple, Mohammed was appointed as the head of the Nation of Islam community in Philadelphia in 1958, when he was 25 years old. There, he introduced the membership to readings from the Koran and other elements of traditional Muslim worship. Two years later, his ministerial career came to a temporary halt after he was convicted of draft evasion. Like his father and many other Black Muslims, Mohammed had refused to serve in the United States military, believing it to be against his religious convictions. For 14 months, between late 1961 and February 1963, Mohammed was an inmate at the Sandstone Federal Correctional Institution in Minnesota.

Doubts, Dissent, and Malcolm X

During his time in prison, Mohammed spent a great deal of time reflecting on his beliefs and on the doubts he had long held about his father's religious message. It was during this period that he came to a life-changing conclusion that he later summed up in these simple words: "Elijah Muhammad was not a prophet." In other words, he accepted the Muslim belief that the final prophet of Allah was Muhammad in the seventh century. In so doing, he converted to the traditional Islamic faith. As a result, he resolved that he would no longer preach about the divinity of Elijah Muhammad and Wallace Dodd Fard, but he did not yet publicly disavow these basic beliefs that were the foundation of the Nation of Islam. Upon his release from prison, he resumed his duties at the temple in Philadelphia.

Warith Mohammed was not the only Black Muslim to have doubts about Elijah Muhammad. Another was Malcolm X, who had joined the movement in the early 1950s and soon became one of the Nation's senior leaders. His electrifying speeches drew many converts to the religion and made him one of the most vocal proponents for African-American rights in the nation. Malcolm X's beliefs underwent a change in the early 1960s and, like Warith Mohammed, he moved toward conventional Islam. His new outlook was partly caused by his loss of faith in Elijah Muhammad after he learned that the leader had fathered numerous children outside his marriage and that he and members of his family had misused the Nation's income to enrich themselves.

Warith Mohammed was also upset at his father's behavior, and he and Malcolm X became closer during this time. In 1964, Mohammed began to

Malcolm X in the early 1960s,
about when he began to question the Nation of Islam.

publicly challenge his father's teachings and leadership. His actions, along with those of Malcolm X, fueled a growing division with the Nation of Islam. In response, Elijah Muhammad temporarily suspended both men from the movement. Shortly thereafter, Malcolm X formally left the Nation of Islam, and the group's leaders viewed this as an unforgivable betrayal. Several violent clashes took place between supporters of Malcolm X and Elijah Muhammad, and numerous public threats were made against Malcolm.

On February 21, 1965, Malcolm X was assassinated while speaking before an audience in Harlem, a section of New York City. The gunmen were three members of the Nation of Islam. Elijah Muhammad denied responsibility for the killing and was never directly linked to the assassins. Nonetheless, many believe that he ordered the shooting. Even if he was not directly involved, his criticism of Malcolm X certainly encouraged extremists to target the former Nation leader.

For Warith Mohammed, the assassination of Malcolm X was a reminder of the dangers that he was facing in deviating from his father's teachings, and the events seemed to convince him to temporarily give up his rebellious position. Less than a week after the assassination, Warith appeared before the Nation of Islam's national convention and publicly asked for forgiveness for questioning Elijah Muhammad. "I judged my father when I should have let God do it," he stated. Years later, he would claim that he rejoined the Nation in the "interest of using my influence to keep them from going to more extremes," but many observers believe he did so because he feared that his own life was on the line.

The Return of the Chosen Son

While no longer in open rebellion against his father's teachings, Warith Mohammed still refused to be completely obedient to Elijah Muhammad. As a result, he was excommunicated, or banished, from the Nation on several different occasions between the mid-1960s and mid-1970s. Each time, he was later reinstated, but his refusal to publicly affirm his father as a prophet meant that he was not allowed to hold a paid position with the movement. He and his family subsisted on the small income he earned from welding, painting, and working other jobs. Meanwhile, he faced ongoing harassment and threats from those who were unhappy with his views.

While Warith Mohammed and Elijah Muhammad were often at odds, the two still maintained a bond with one another. "When he put me out of the Nation, he did it in a way to make me feel that he wished he didn't have to do it," Warith explained. "I had no bad feelings for him." In addition, Warith continued to be viewed by many as the so-called chosen son, and that status may have been part of the reason that he was able to challenge his father in certain ways. "Because they said I was special person, that freed me up to criticize, to question things," Mohammed noted.

Elijah Muhammad's growing tolerance of his son's views became clear in 1974, when Warith Mohammed was given permission to resume preaching in Nation of Islam mosques. Moreover, Warith was allowed to proclaim his mainstream Islamic teachings, which did not uphold the divinity of his father and Fard. With this development, Warith was recognized as a lead-

Mohammed greets followers at Saviours' Day services in Chicago on February 26, 1975, the day after the death of his father.

ing candidate to succeed Elijah Muhammad. The question of who would next head the movement was becoming increasingly urgent at this point because Elijah Muhammad—then in his mid-70s—was in poor health. On February 25, 1975, he passed away. The following day, Warith Mohammed was recognized as the new supreme minister of the Nation of Islam.

Reforming a Religious Movement

Almost immediately, Mohammed began to make important changes to the religious group his father had built. To help heal the wounds caused by past disputes in the organization, he disbanded the Fruit of Islam security force and renamed the New York City mosque in honor of Malcolm X. He relaxed the strict dress code that had been in place for decades, and he sold many of the Nation's businesses to pay overdue taxes and settle other debts. While Elijah Muhammad had ruled over a highly centralized organization, Warith Mohammed began to allow local mosques more control over their own affairs, and he no longer required them to contribute money to the organization's headquarters. Ultimately, the religious movement he headed became a loosely connected association of mosques that looked to Mohammed for guidance but were not held to strict rules. Around 1977, he decided to signify the group's new direction by renaming it the World Community of Al-Islam in the West, and it was at this point that he changed his own name to Warith Deen Mohammed. The religious organization later took on a succession of other titles, the best known being the Muslim American Society.

—— " ——

When Mohammed became the supreme minister of the Nation of Islam, he abandoned some of the group's core beliefs, including the Nation's teachings about the evils of white people. "It's time for us to stop calling white folks the devil," he proclaimed, "because there's some black devils, too."

—— " ——

Some of the most startling changes for members had to do with the religious beliefs that had been the core of the Nation of Islam's theology. Mohammed publicly renounced his father as a prophet and began to lead the movement's members toward the principles of Sunni Islam. He urged followers to pray five times each day, to learn Arabic, and to study the Koran. Perhaps most strikingly, the Nation of Islam teachings about the evils of whites were abandoned, and the movement even began accepting non-blacks as members. "It's time for us to stop calling white folks the devil," Mohammed proclaimed, "because there's some black devils, too."

In the span of a few years, Mohammed overhauled a religious group that had been in existence for more than four decades. Given the scope of the changes he introduced, he ran the risk that many members would abandon the movement. He also faced the possibility that his reforms would spark violent battles between rival factions, as had happened previously in the Nation's history. For several years, he was able to keep the movement unified, but in the late 1970s, a figure stepped forward to oppose his reforms.

Louis Farrakhan and the "New" Nation of Islam

In the years before Elijah Muhammad's death, Warith Mohammed had been just one of several people who were considered as possible successors. Another was Louis Farrakhan, the head of the Nation of Islam's Harlem mosque in New York City and the movement's national spokesperson. When Warith Mohammed became supreme minister in 1975, Farrakhan initially pledged his support, but his loyalty was short-lived. In 1978, Farrakhan began reviving the original race-based teachings of the Nation of Islam, and he formally broke away from Mohammed's movement the following year to start his own religious group. Farrakhan called his organization the Nation of Islam, and the revival of the old name was fitting. In essence, Farrakhan's group continued the original spiritual beliefs that had been established by Elijah Muhammad. Farrakhan maintained that Wallace Dodd Fard was Allah in human form, that Elijah Muhammad was a prophet, and that whites were an evil, inferior race.

Farrakhan and Mohammed were now rivals, and the two men would engage in a war of words for more than 20 years. Their conflict never escalated beyond verbal attacks, however. Unlike previous divisions in the movement, this clash did not lead to violence and killings, and the lack of bloodshed was another testament to the new direction Mohammed was forging. He refused to use force to strengthen his hold on power.

With the division between Mohammed and Farrakhan, the movement's members were forced to choose which leader and beliefs they would follow. Judged on this account, Mohammed's organization proved more popular, as it is believed to have a much larger membership than Farrakhan's Nation of Islam does. A study by the Council on American-Islamic Relations in the early 2000s found that two-thirds of the mosques in the United States that were predominantly African American were affiliated with Mohammed's organization, with the remainder divided between the Nation of Islam and several other organizations. The exact number of people that belong to these groups is unknown, however, and estimates vary considerably. The total membership of Mohammed's association in the mid-2000s has been estimated by some sources to be as small as 50,000 while others put it at around two million.

In terms of public perception, however, Farrakhan emerged as the better known leader. This was largely the result of his teachings about black supremacy and his statements against the Jewish people, both of which drew a great deal of media attention. In 1995, he played a leading role in the Million Man March in Washington DC, which drew together blacks from all across the country, though not all of them endorsed Farrakhan's controversial ideas. Mohammed condemned the Million Man March as a moneymaking scheme by Farrakhan, and he continually criticized the divisive and confrontational stance of his rival. "Farrakhan is working from a position of anger, and I'm working from a position of peace," he asserted in the mid-1990s. In another interview, he characterized Farrakhan's teachings as negative influences that have "taken our people further and further into darkness."

Mohammed in 1992, with a portrait of his father.

A Voice of Moderation

The division between Mohammed and Farrakhan reflected a larger debate among African Americans: the degree to which they should focus on the legacy of racial injustice experienced by blacks in the United States. In Mohammed's view, African Americans were enjoying new opportunities by the turn of the 21st century, and he felt it was time to give up what he regarded as "an emotional rage directed at the past." This was part of the reason that he opposed Farrakhan's continuation of his father's teachings. "The Nation was designed to attract poor and hopeless blacks to come to something created for nobody but them," he noted in 2001. "But we live in new realities now.... Blacks are being encouraged to aspire to the highest positions in America now. Everything is open to us. There is very little place for the extreme idea of the Nation of Islam in America today."

Not surprisingly, this message was better received by African Americans who had achieved a certain degree of financial security, while more militant views, such as those expressed by Farrakhan, proved more popular with blacks who suffered hardship. Consequently, the followers of Mohammed's Islamic association, on the, have tended to belong to the middle class, while Farrakhan's Nation of Islam has enjoyed its strongest support in poor inner-city areas—the same locations that had been the stronghold of the Nation under Elijah Muhammad.

In keeping with his moderate views, Warith Mohammed also voiced strong support for the existing political values and institutions of the United States—a striking contrast with his father's belief that blacks should have a nation unto themselves. Mohammed believed this acceptance was justified because of the tremendous social changes that had taken place in the country since the mid-1900s, stating that "we should love America passionately now that America has changed so drastically within a relatively short time." The same man who once refused to serve in the armed forces did away with the anti-military tenets of the old Nation of Islam, and the U.S. flag was prominently displayed in the mosques of his organization.

Mohammed's patriotic views defied the stereotypical image of Muslims as being anti-American, and his stance helped demonstrate that Islam includes a wide range of people with differing views. In the wake of the terrorist attacks on September 11, 2001, he strongly supported the U.S. military invasion of Afghanistan, stating that "the government should go wherever there is oppression of human beings and show them the way. My only regret is that I'm not the president. I would like to take the Army there myself." In addition, he used many of his post-9/11 interviews to fight against the perception that Muslims approved of violent extremism. "Terrorism has no place in Islam," he said, "just as it has no place in Christianity or Judaism."

A World Leader

During his decades of leadership, Mohammed began receiving greater recognition from political leaders and from religious authorities from other faiths. In 1992, he became the first Muslim leader to deliver a prayer and invocation before the U.S. Senate. "It felt for the first time that I was going to be free in America," he said of that event. "It was a sign of being accepted." In addition, he was invited to take part in the 1993 and 1997 inaugurations of President Clinton as a representative of America's Muslim citizens.

An increasingly prominent figure on the world stage, Mohammed frequently met with officials from other faiths. In 1996, he led a delegation of Muslims to Rome to consult with Pope John Paul II, and he made a second appearance at the Vatican in 1999. He also became the first Muslim to address the general assembly of the National Council of Churches. Mohammed received great respect from the worldwide Muslim community as well, and he enjoyed an especially close relationship with the government of Saudi Arabia. Their ties reached back to the late 1970s, and for a number of years Mohammed's religious movement received financial support from the Saudis. This funding ended in the mid-1990s, according to Mohammed, because he refused to support the Saudi's position on certain international issues.

Mohammed made use of his contacts in the Muslim world to create new business opportunities for the members of his association. A partnership was formed with several Islamic nations that allowed members of the Muslim American Society to purchase international goods at a discount for resale in the United States. This was part of his organization's ongoing efforts to assist in the creation of black-owned businesses. The most prominent of these endeavors was the Collective Purchasing Conference, later known as CPC/Comtrust, which allowed small investors to pool their resources to improve their buying power.

Reaching Out to a Rival

Public speeches were a common part of Warith Mohammed's life, but the appearance he made at the McCormick Center in Chicago on February 26, 1999, stood apart from the rest. On that day, he spoke at the annual Saviours' Day gathering of the Nation of Islam—the group headed by his longtime rival Louis Farrakhan. Mohammed's appearance at the event signified an attempt at mending the 21-year old division between his Muslim American Society and Farrakhan's followers, and in his speech he endorsed unity and brotherhood among all Muslims. The following year, the reconciliation went a step farther. Farrakhan and Mohammed publicly embraced at the 2000 Saviours' Day event, and Farrakhan stated that "we will be together as a family.... Not for evil, but for love—not hatred, but in good."

This development came about as Farrakhan's group moved closer to the mainstream Islamic practices and beliefs that Mohammed had adopted years before. Farrakhan's health was also reportedly a motivating factor, as his battle with prostate cancer in the late 1990s had convinced him to promote unity. Mohammed welcomed the improved relations and later remarked that "it is very clear to me that Minister Farrakhan and the Nation of Islam are very serious in embracing the love and peace message of Islam and putting the harsh rhetoric behind." In the years that followed, the two groups have generally been on good terms with one another, but there has been little progress toward officially unifying into one organization. At times in the 2000s, Mohammed and Farrakhan even resumed their criticisms of one another, though their attacks were less frequent and less antagonistic than in decades past.

*Mohammed embraces Louis Farrakhan at the
Nation of Islam Saviours' Day gathering, 2000.*

Final Years

In September 2003, as he approached his 70th birthday, Warith Mohammed resigned as the head of the American Society of Muslims, a move that was partly inspired by his wish to reduce his responsibilities. "When I told the imams [Muslim religious leaders] about my resignation," he noted, "a big burden went off my back." In addition, he confessed that his decision to step down came partly out of the frustration that he felt toward some of the local imams who were part of the association. "I have tried over the last 10 to 12 years to encourage them to get more religious education, but I have made no progress. They want their followers to just obey them, but not to question them or right their wrongs."

95

Even though he gave up his official position, Mohammed still served as an influential religious authority for many African-American Muslims. He remained a prominent public figure as well, delivering sermons, speeches, and interviews, and he also devoted himself to Mosque Cares, a charity organization he had founded. His busy schedule continued through the final weeks of his life, and when he passed away at his home in Markham, Illinois, on September 9, 2008, the loss took many of his followers by surprise. His death at age 74 was attributed to heart disease and complications from diabetes. Some 8,000 of his friends and followers attended his funeral.

At the time of Mohammed's passing, many people commented on the surprising transition that he was able to achieve in convincing thousands of African Americans to accept Sunni Muslim beliefs. "I don't think people understand the tremendous change that occurred when he made that move," noted Lawrence Mamiya, a professor of religion at Vassar College, who was quoted in the *Chicago Tribune*. "He moved people from that concept of black nationalism into universal consciousness of the faith." Abdullah El-Amin, the head of Muslim Center in Detroit, echoed that idea in the *Detroit Free Press*, stating that Mohammed "was a reviver of the religion.... He brought a whole lot of people to the correct worship of Islam."

Others focused on Mohammed's role as a mediator who reached out to other faiths. Quoted in the *New Journal and Guide*, Imam Muhammad Asadi of Virginia voiced the opinion that "W. D. Mohammed's legacy as a human being was to bring humanity together and use truth and understanding to build bridges." The ideal of finding common spiritual ground with others was a continuing priority for Mohammed, particularly in the later decades of his life. When asked to sum up his goals in a 2001 interview, Mohammed did so by linking his faith to other major religions. "My dream is the same as (the dreams of) faithful and loving Jewish, Christian, and Buddhist leaders," he affirmed. "Our dream is the dream of scripture.... We want to see human society be the best it can possibly be."

HOME AND FAMILY

The details of Warith Mohammed's family life are not well known. At the time of his death, he was married to Khadija Mohammed, and he had been wed three times previously and had married one of his wives on two separate occasions. Some sources indicate that he had nine children while others cite eight, and he had five stepchildren. He was a longtime resident of the Chicago area, living his final years in the suburb of Markham. He also had a second residence in Little Rock, Arkansas.

In his later years Mohammed served as an influential religious leader and spoke at many different types of gatherings, including this lecture at the University of Arkansas Clinton School of Public Service in Little Rock, Arkansas.

SELECTED WRITINGS

The Man and the Woman in Islam, 1976
The Teachings of W. D. Muhammad, 1976
Prayer and Al-Islam, 1982
Religion on the Line, 1983
Imam W. Deen Muhammad Speaks from Harlem, N.Y., 1984
An African American Genesis, 1986
Al-Islam Unity and Leadership, 1991
Islam's Climate for Business Success, 1995
The Champion We have in Common: The Dynamic African American Soul, 2002

HONORS AND AWARDS

100 Most Influential African Americans in the World (*Ebony* magazine): 2000 and 2001
Ghandi King Ikeda Award for Peace (Morehouse College): 2002

Hall of Honor Inductee (Martin Luther King Jr. International Chapel): 2002
Honorary Doctorate of Humane Letters (Sojourner-Douglass College): 2003
Outstanding Leadership Award (Council on American-Islamic Relations):
   2005

FURTHER READING

Books

Blake, John. *Children of the Movement,* 2004
Britannica Biographies, 2008
Evanzz, Karl. *The Judas Factor: The Plot to Kill Malcolm X,* 1992
Who's Who among African Americans, 2008

Periodicals

Chicago Tribune, Sep. 10, 2008
Current Biography Yearbook, 2004
Detroit Free Press, Sep. 10, 2008
Islamic Horizons, July/Aug. 2005
Los Angeles Times, May 15, 1999, p.2; July 8, 2000, p.2
Middle East, Sept. 2001, p.19
Tampa Tribune, Feb. 16, 1997, p.1
Washington Post, Sep. 10, 2008, p.B7
Wilson Quarterly, Autumn 2005, p.16

Online Articles

http://www.csmonitor.com/2002/0214/p03s01-ussc.htm
   (Christian Science Monitor, "America's Black Muslims Close a Rift," Feb.
   14, 2002)
http://www.pbs.org/thisfarbyfaith/people/warith_deen_mohammed.html
   (PBS, This Far by Faith, "Warith Deen Mohammed," 2003)
http://www.njournalg.com/NoReplacementForthcoming.htm
   (New Journal and Guide, "No Replacement Forthcoming for Esteemed
   Leader," Sep. 17, 2008)

WORLD WIDE WEB SITE

http://www.ar-razzaq.org/MosqueCares

Suze Orman 1951-

American Financial Advisor and Television Commentator
Bestselling Author and Host of CNBC's "The Suze Orman Show"

BIRTH

Suze (pronounced "Suzie," short for Susan) Orman was born on June 5, 1951, in Chicago, Illinois. She was the youngest of three children of Morry Orman, a store owner and business-man, and Ann Orman, a legal secretary. They raised Suze and her two older brothers on the south side of Chicago, where the family ran a chicken take-out shop.

YOUTH

Orman's parents had emigrated from Russia, and they struggled at times to make ends meet. "The shame, fear, and anger I felt growing up ... as poor little Suze Orman from the south side of Chicago, daughter of a chicken plucker, defined me well into adulthood," she remembered in her book *The Courage to Be Rich.* "No matter how well I did or how much money I made, I never felt good enough, smart enough, attractive enough." Her self-esteem was further weakened during elementary school, where she struggled with reading because of a speech problem. When a teacher decided to seat her class by their scores on a reading exam, "my three best friends [were] in the first three seats of the first row, while I was banished to the last seat in the sixth row," Orman recalled. "If I always secretly felt dumb, it was now officially confirmed for everyone to see."

> "The shame, fear, and anger I felt growing up ... as poor little Suze Orman from the south side of Chicago, daughter of a chicken plucker, defined me well into adulthood. No matter how well I did or how much money I made, I never felt good enough, smart enough, attractive enough."

To make matters worse, her parents suffered a series of financial setbacks that affected the entire family. When Orman was 13, a fire destroyed the chicken take-out shop her family owned. She watched as her father ran back into the burning building to save the cash register, which held all the family's earnings. "When he threw the register on the ground, the skin on his arms and chest came with it," she recalled. "That was when I learned that money is obviously more important than life itself." The family couldn't afford insurance, so they had to rebuild from scratch. Morry Orman recovered from his burns and opened a deli in downtown Chicago, but then was sued by a woman paralyzed at a boarding house he owned with his father. To help make ends meet, Ann Orman took a full-time job as a legal secretary, which was unusual for a mother at the time. To help out, Suze and her brothers often worked in the family store or at odd jobs.

Although Orman worried about measuring up to her classmates, it didn't slow her down in high school. She was very involved in school activities, joining a dozen clubs and serving on several school committees. There were no organized sports for girls, so she and her many friends often let off steam by playing "hide-and-seek tag" at Chicago's famous Museum of Science and Industry. Because she felt she wasn't as smart as her fellow students, she didn't try to get top grades; still, she planned to attend college after she finished high school.

EDUCATION

After graduating from Chicago's South Shore High School in 1969, Orman enrolled at the University of Illinois. Although she hoped to become a brain surgeon, a guidance counselor discouraged her because of her average grades and test scores. Instead, she majored in social work. She worked her way through college and shared a house with a couple of friends, one of whom was future comedy superstar John Belushi. Orman was scheduled to graduate in 1973, but she failed to complete a foreign language requirement and left school to travel around the country. Several years later, she completed the needed courses at a school in California and received her bachelor's degree from the University of Illinois in 1976.

CAREER HIGHLIGHTS

A Rocky Road to Success

After leaving school in 1973, Orman borrowed enough money from her brother to buy a van. She and three friends drove across country and ended up in California. In Berkeley, she got a job cutting and clearing dead trees and lived in her van for a few months. Eventually she settled down and found a job as a waitress at the Buttercup Bakery. Orman worked there for nearly seven years, until she decided she wanted to open her own restaurant. She had little savings of her own to start a business, however, and her parents couldn't afford to help her out. It was her regular customers at the Buttercup who ended up lending her the seed money to start her own business.

Orman's customers were able to lend her $50,000. But that wasn't enough to start a business from scratch, so one customer recommended she take the money to invest with a stockbroker at the local Merrill Lynch office. Knowing little about financial markets, Orman trusted the broker there to handle her money properly. "I did exactly what he asked, never thinking that it was stupid or dangerous for me to sign blank papers," she recalled. Instead of putting her money in something conservative, like a money market account, the broker put it into a high-risk investment. For the first couple of weeks the gamble paid off and Orman made a lot of money. Then the markets changed, and after three months she had lost everything.

*Despite the financial difficulties she faced early in life,
Orman went on to become a respected expert on financial issues.*

Orman knew she couldn't make enough money to pay back her loans on
her waitress's salary of $400 a month. She had been studying the stock
market and figured she couldn't do any worse than her first advisor. She
walked into Merrill Lynch and asked for a job interview. Although she did-
n't know how to dress for business and had no financial experience, they
gave her a job. During her first days there, Orman felt like she had in
school—like she wasn't smart enough to belong—but she studied hard to
take her stockbroker's exam. During her studies, she discovered that the
broker who had lost her money had broken the rules. Although she
thought it might jeopardize her job, she decided to sue the Merrill Lynch
office where she was working.

Orman didn't know that Merrill Lynch couldn't fire someone who was
suing them, so she kept her job despite the lawsuit. During the months it
took to litigate the case, Orman earned her stockbroker's qualifications
and became one of her office's top sellers. Merrill Lynch ended up settling
the lawsuit out of court, giving her enough money to pay back her friends
at the Buttercup. In the meantime, she was earning a six-figure salary, partly by taking on unconventional clients, like low- and middle-income wait-
resses and truck drivers. She remained at Merrill Lynch until 1983, when
she traveled to India and Nepal to study meditation and explore spirituali-

ty. When she returned to California, she took a job with Prudential Bache Securities, eventually becoming vice-president of investments. In 1987 she went into business for herself, creating the Suze Orman Financial Group and working as a Certified Financial Planner.

Learning Lessons from Loss

Orman had won many clients with her bubbly personality and personal service, and she planned on taking them with her into her new business. She had barely set up shop when an assistant stole all her records, both paper files and computer programs. Orman tried to keep the business going, but she was forced to resort to credit card debt to maintain appearances. Soon she owed almost $250,000 and had reached the limits of her credit; she also became depressed. She sued her assistant for $500,000, but was only awarded $6,000 in damages. She couldn't even collect the money after the woman declared bankruptcy. Despite these troubles, Orman found a valuable lesson in the experience. She decided to forgive the woman and claimed responsibility for her part in the dispute. "I apologized to that woman," she explained. "I needed to learn the lesson that money can't buy happiness. Even with my spiritual quest, I thought I was better than people because I had money."

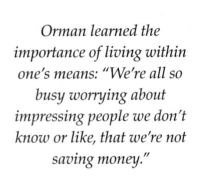

Orman learned the importance of living within one's means: "We're all so busy worrying about impressing people we don't know or like, that we're not saving money."

With a new attitude toward money and lots of hard work, Orman rebuilt her business. Within three years she had repaid her debts and was once again on the path to success. She felt the need to share the lessons she had learned and began "telling everyone I knew what had happened to me," she explained. "The more I opened up, the happier I felt." In 1995 she published *You've Earned It, Don't Lose It,* a book based on her experiences and a retirement seminar she had developed. *You've Earned It, Don't Lose It* was geared towards lower- and middle-income people who can't afford to lose any of their hard-earned savings. It stressed protecting money, rather than trying to grow it. Orman opened each chapter with story of a financial mistake, then showed how the mistake could have been prevented. She covered a broad range of important financial subjects: insurance, wills and inheritances, retirement issues, and legal and medical troubles that can affect a person's finances.

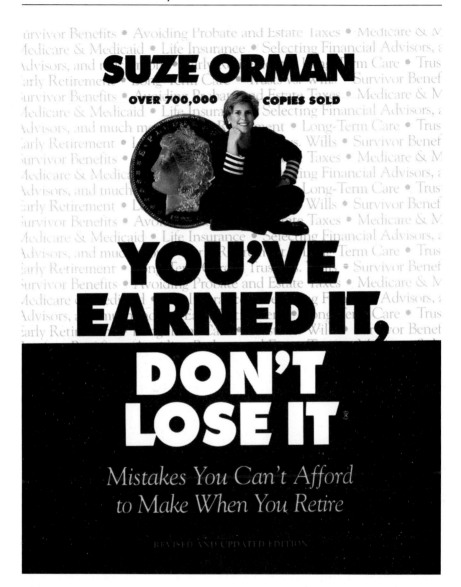

You've Earned it, Don't Lose It *was Orman's first published book.*

Orman worked hard with her publisher to promote the book and eventually convinced QVC, a television shopping channel, to give her time to sell it. In that first segment, aired October 1995, she sold all 2,500 copies they had in stock. Three months later, on Super Bowl Sunday, she sold 10,000 copies in just 12 minutes. Eventually, Orman sold over 700,000 copies of *You've Earned It, Don't Lose It.* She also became a featured vendor on QVC, hosting the channel's "Financial Freedom Hour" beginning in 1996.

To help sales of her first book, Orman toured the country to sign copies in different cities. During one of those signings she met a producer from a local Public Broadcasting System (PBS) television station. The producer suggested she appear during the station's next pledge drive to sell her book and help the station raise money. When Orman published her second book, *The 9 Steps to Financial Freedom* (1997), she created a TV program of the same title to be broadcast on PBS stations nationwide. Orman toured 21 stations around the country and helped the network raise more than $2.3 million, their most successful fundraiser to that point.

Orman's career in broadcasting really took off after she began appearing on "The Oprah Winfrey Show." She first appeared as a guest in January 1998. After several more visits to the show, *The 9 Steps to Financial Freedom* topped the *New York Times* list of best-selling nonfiction. In the book, Orman again used real-life stories to illustrate how people let their feelings about money get in the way of using it wisely. She emphasized dealing with your emotional responses to money as part of a sound financial plan. "Money will not set you free," she explained. "It's your control over your thoughts and fears about money that will set you free." *The 9 Steps* became her biggest-selling book, with over 3.1 million copies in print.

Becoming a Media Superstar

Orman also reached the top of the best-seller list with her next book, *The Courage to Be Rich* (1999), which sold 1.2 million copies. She wrote the book, she said, after seeing many of her friends get divorced over money issues. "A lot of them were treating their money the exact same way they treated their relationship: in essence, they weren't quite honest. So I started to realize that the way we related to people was the exact same way we related to money." Again, she used real-life examples to show ways to deal with marriage, divorce, and death without letting money issues complicate things. Her 2001 book *The Road to Wealth* was another chart-topper, selling more than 660,000 copies. It was designed as a one-stop reference for all kinds of financial questions. The book was so successful that Orman brought out an updated version in 2008.

Even as she conquered the best-seller charts, Orman was finding more ways to reach an audience. She continued as a regular guest on "The Oprah Winfrey Show" and also made appearances on NBC's "Today" morning show and the news network CNN. She also brought out a DVD

Many of Orman's popular books were made into DVDs also, expanding her reach.

to accompany each new book, and soon Orman was answering questions on her own radio show. Then "The Suze Orman Show" debuted on cable financial network CNBC in March 2002. The "Can I Afford It?" segment became very popular, as viewers called in to ask whether they could afford various items—from designer jeans to luxury cars. After listening to their financial information, Orman would shout, "Approved!" or "Denied!"

Orman continued hitting the best-seller charts with finance books that offered advice for different times and different groups. The 2003 book *The Laws of Money, The Lessons of Life* was written after the terrorist attacks on 9/11 ended the economic boom of the 1990s. It focused on how to deal with difficult financial times and offered the advice to "look at what you have, not at what you had." *The Money Book for the Young, Fabulous, & Broke,* published in 2005, focused on money issues important to people in their 20s: car payments, taxes, student loans, and how to save and invest money. Orman suggested the most important thing for young people is to establish and maintain good credit, because people with good credit pay less interest. She also suggested young workers focus on jobs that provide the best chance for advancement, rather than the best salary. She stressed the importance of living within one's means: "We're all so busy worrying about impressing people we don't know or like, that we're not saving money."

Orman tailored her advice to women in the 2007 book *Women & Money: Owning the Power to Control Your Destiny.* She encouraged women to save for their own future rather than spend their money solely on others. Although women might have the reputation of being thrifty, "they save and then they give it to their best friends, who need it," Orman commented. "They give it to their children, who need it. They give it all away once they've saved it." She added, "I want to change women from savers to investors." To further the cause of educating women about finances, in 2008 she become a consultant to Avon, the in-home cosmetics company that employs almost half a million women in the U.S. alone.

In 2009 Orman published a new book, *Suze Orman's 2009 Action Plan.* Given the stock market freefall, the credit crunch, the drop in the housing market and the many home foreclosures, and the steep rise in unemployment, Orman felt the need to publish timely information that's relevant to today's economic conditions. *Suze Orman's 2009 Action Plan* is a one-time book targeted to help people deal with the recent economic crisis and take advantage of new laws and tax breaks that have been passed in response to the crisis. It helps readers develop action plans for dealing with such issues as the credit market, savings and spending, real estate, and paying for college. The book is for sale in stores and other locations, but it was also offered as a free download from oprah.com when it was first published.

In addition to selling millions of books and DVDs, Orman has also created financial kits and sold them through her web site. Various kits show people how to check and fix their credit, develop a will or trust, buy necessary insurance, and avoid identity theft. She is also a very popular public speaker who has lectured to many groups around the country, including a 2005 tour with hip-hop mogul Russell Simmons to promote financial planning for urban youth. Orman has won numerous awards for her work, including two Emmys for her television show. In 2008, *Time* magazine named her one of the 100 most influential people in the world. Orman has become so famous that she even inspired several skits on the comedy program "Saturday Night Live." She has said that she doesn't mind being the subject of a spoof: "One of those times I was in the audience," she recalled. "By all means, if they ever ask me [to appear on the show], it would be one of the greatest honors of my life."

> *Orman makes financial advice entertaining, which helps everyday people understand important issues. According to critic Henry Goldblatt, "Her boisterous delivery is so compelling that it doesn't matter if she's spouting off about variable life insurance or reciting [Russian literature]. She's just a blast to be around."*

Response to Her Work

Orman has had her share of critics. Some have called her advice too conservative and one-size-fits-all. Others have faulted her endorsement of certain financial products. Orman has responded that she only promotes products she believes in and doesn't receive any money for her recommendations. (She earns enough from her own businesses; observers estimate she is worth around $25 million.) To critics who call her advice overly simplistic, she has said, "get out there and talk to people like I do. The truth is, they haven't got any money. Who has money to invest anymore? Invest what?" Others have faulted her emphasis on emotional issues, but Orman noted that "even though I'm the last person to say money will buy happiness—because it won't—I'll be the first to say the lack of money will make you miserable." She believes that in dealing with financial issues, the

Orman has become so famous that she was even a subject of parody on "Saturday Night Live," including this skit featuring Kristen Wiig.

focus should be on "people first, then money, then things." Her ability to make financial advice entertaining helps everyday people understand important issues. As critic Henry Goldblatt wrote in *Entertainment Weekly*, "Her boisterous delivery is so compelling that it doesn't matter if she's spouting off about variable life insurance or reciting [Russian literature]. She's just a blast to be around."

Many would argue that Orman's advice is appealing because it is full of common sense: avoid credit card debt; contribute as much as possible to a 401(k) retirement savings account to get matching funds from your employer; and use any extra money to pay off auto loans and other debts before putting it into investments. She also advocates spending within one's means and warns against hiding money from a spouse. Finally, she stresses the importance of learning everything possible about your loans and investments—never just sign an empty form and trust your finances to someone else. While this advice has been common for years, she has an ability to describe it in terms a non-expert can understand.

Orman's enthusiasm and communication skills are a great part of her success. She takes a subject many people find boring or confusing and relates it to everyday experiences. She encourages people to separate feelings of shame and guilt from how they handle money. "The time has come for each and every one of us when our self-worth has to mean more than our net worth," she declared. Most important, she noted, is for people to take charge of their own finances. "Power doesn't come from relying on someone else to handle your money. It is created when you—and only you—take the initiative to learn about your money and to make sure that you have what you need."

"Power doesn't come from relying on someone else to handle your money. It is created when you—and only you—take the initiative to learn about your money and to make sure that you have what you need."

HOME AND FAMILY

Even after becoming a best-selling author, Orman kept the small house in Oakland Hills, California, that she bought when she was waitress. Later she moved to Pacific Heights, in the San Francisco area. She has also purchased a small apartment (only 900 square feet) in New York City and a home in Florida, which is her official residence. She also owns a home in South Africa, where she has expanded her consulting business. All four of her homes are completely paid off, with no debt attached to them.

In 2007, Orman came out as a lesbian, acknowledging her long-time partner, Kathy "K.T." Travis, a marketing executive who now works for Orman's company. She hopes that someday they can be legally married. "It's killing me that upon my death, K.T. is going to lose 50 percent of everything I have to [pay] estate taxes, or vice versa."

HOBBIES AND OTHER INTERESTS

Orman takes time from her busy schedule to practice Siddha yoga meditation. She also spends considerable time and money on behalf of charity. She devoted a chapter on charitable giving to *The Courage to Be Rich* and believes by sending money into the world, you won't feel poor and "your demeanor will be instead expansive and open, ready to receive." She donates around one-quarter of her income to charity, especially religious, environmental, and women's groups. The National Multiple Sclerosis Society gave her their first MS Spirit Award in 2006 for her support of the organization.

Orman also donates her services to worthy groups. She participated in "Military Saves" week by giving speeches and free copies of her books to military families. During the financial crisis of 2008, she donated her to time to create public service announcements for the Federal Deposit Insurance Corporation (FDIC), assuring people their money was safe in banks.

WRITING AND TELEVISION CREDITS

Books

You've Earned It, Don't Lose It, 1995, revised edition, 1999 (with Linda Mead)
The 9 Steps to Financial Freedom, 1997
Suze Orman's Financial Guidebook, 1998
The Courage to Be Rich, 1999
The Road to Wealth, 2001; revised edition, 2008
The Laws of Money, the Lessons of Life, 2003
The Money Book for the Young, Fabulous & Broke, 2005
Women & Money: Owning the Power to Control Your Destiny, 2007
Suze Orman's 2009 Action Plan: Keeping Your Money Safe and Sound, 2009

Television

"Financial Freedom Hour," 1996-
"The 9 Steps to Financial Freedom," 1997
"The Courage to Be Rich," 1999
"The Road to Wealth," 2001
"The Suze Orman Show," 2002-
"Suze Orman: The Laws of Money, the Lessons of Life," 2003
"Suze Orman: for the Young, Fabulous & Broke," 2005
"Women & Money: Owning the Power to Control Your Destiny," 2007
Also makes regular appearances on "The Oprah Winfrey Show," "Larry King Live," "The View," and "Today."

HONORS AND AWARDS

Books for a Better Life Award (National Multiple Sclerosis Society): 1999, Motivational Award, for *The Courage to Be Rich;* 2003, Hall of Fame induction
Luminaries Award (TJFR Group News): 2002, for lifetime achievement in business journalism
Crossing Borders Award (Feminist Press): 2003
Gracie Allen Award (American Women in Radio & Television): 2003, for Outstanding National/Network/Syndication Talk Show; 2005, for Individual Achievement Award as Outstanding Program Host; 2006, for Individual Achievement Award as Outstanding Program Host; 2007, for

Outstanding Talk Show, all for "The Suze Orman Show"; 2008, for Outstanding Talk Show, all for "The Suze Orman Show"
Daytime Emmy Awards (National Academy of Television Arts and Sciences): 2004, for Outstanding Service Show Host, for "Suze Orman: The Lessons of Money, The Lessons of Life," 2006, for Outstanding Service Show Host, for "Suze Orman: For the Young, Fabulous & Broke"
Multiple Sclerosis Spirit Award (National Multiple Sclerosis Society): 2006
National Equality Award (Human Rights Campaign): 2008
Amelia Earhart Award (Crittenton Women's Union): 2008
CableFAX Program Award (CableFAX magazine): 2008, for Best Show or Series in the Talk Show/ Commentary, for "The Suze Orman Show"

FURTHER READING

Books

Orman, Suze. *The Courage to Be Rich,* 1999

Periodicals

American Prospect, Dec. 2007, p.35
Biography, Apr. 2001, p.62
Current Biography Yearbook, 2003
Entertainment Weekly, Sep. 12, 2008, p.125
Fortune, June 16, 2003, p.82
Kiplinger's Personal Finance Magazine, Nov. 1998, p.96
Minneapolis Star-Tribune, Aug. 3, 2001, p.E1
New York Times, Mar. 18, 2007, p.BU7
New York Times Magazine, Feb. 25, 2007, p.L19
People, May 17, 1999, p.153
Publishers Weekly, Feb. 24, 2003, p.41
Sales & Marketing Management, Aug. 1999, p.120
San Francisco Chronicle, Oct. 25, 2008, p.C1
Self, Dec. 1997, p.114
USA Today, Mar. 21, 2005, p.B6; Mar. 19, 2007, p.B9
Wall Street Journal, Oct. 17, 2008, p.B4

Online Articles

http://www.chicagomag.com/Chicago-Magazine/February-2007/Before-They-Were-Famous
(Chicago Magazine, "Before They Were Famous," Feb. 2007)
http://www.oprah.com/article/omagazine/suze_orman
(O, The Oprah Magazine, "Suze Orman: Personal Finance Expert," undated)

http://www.oprah.com/article/oprahshow/20081119_tows_bookdownload
   (oprah.com, "The Oprah Winfrey Show," undated)
http:www.time.com
   (Time.com, "The 2008 Time 100: The World's Most Influential People,"
   undated)

ADDRESS

Suze Orman
"The Suze Orman Show"
CNBC
900 Sylvan Avenue
Englewood Cliffs, NJ 07632

WORLD WIDE WEB SITES

http://www.suzeorman.com
http://www.cnbc.com

Chris Paul 1985-

American Professional Basketball Player with the
New Orleans Hornets
2005-06 NBA Rookie of the Year
Member of the 2008 Olympic Gold Medal-Winning
USA Men's Basketball Team

BIRTH

Christopher Emmanuel Paul was born on May 6, 1985, in
Winston-Salem, North Carolina. His father, Charles Paul, built
surveillance equipment, while his mother, Robin Paul, over-
saw the technical staff at a bank. Chris has one brother, C.J.,
who is two years older.

YOUTH

Chris Paul grew up in a modest, two-story brick house in the town of Lewisville, about 10 miles from Winston-Salem. His parents had strict rules and expected their boys to follow them. "We went to church, got whuppings when we were bad, and couldn't play our video games during the week," C.J. Paul remembered. "Some people would say it was a rough childhood, but it brought out the best in us. We were raised to give back and never take things for granted."

Throughout his youth, Paul spent a lot of time with his maternal grandfather, Nathaniel Jones, whom he called Papa Chilly. Papa Chilly owned a local gas station, Jones Chevron. When he opened the business in 1964, at the height of the African-American civil rights movement, it was the first black-owned service station in North Carolina. Chris and his brother C.J. worked there during the summer and on weekends. They cleaned windshields, pumped gas, and helped out with routine car maintenance like changing oil and rotating tires. They also learned from their grandfather's example. "My grandfather always worked hard. He took care of my family spiritually, emotionally, and financially," Chris explained. "My granddad was my best friend. I wouldn't be in the position I'm in now had it not been for him and the things he instilled in me—hard work and the importance of family."

> "My grandfather always worked hard. He took care of my family spiritually, emotionally, and financially," Chris explained. "My granddad was my best friend. I wouldn't be in the position I'm in now had it not been for him and the things he instilled in me— hard work and the importance of family."

When he was not going to school or working at the gas station, Chris loved to play sports. Even as a boy, he was very competitive and hated to lose. He and his brother developed a fierce sibling rivalry that extended to all sorts of contests, from basketball and football to bowling and board games. "We didn't finish most of our games, that's how bad it would get," C.J. admitted. "Sometimes my mother would leave work early, just so she could control us." Even though Chris was younger and smaller, he never questioned whether he could compete with C.J. and his friends. "He's always said, 'If they can do it, I'm going to do it,'" Robin Paul noted. "He's always had that determined spirit."

*When Paul was just in high school, he played on the
2003 Jordan Capital Classic Team. Paul is shown in the front row,
third from right; Michael Jordan is in the center.*

Chris Paul showed athletic talent from an early age. He played quarterback in Pop Warner youth football, for example, and led his team to the 10-and-under national championship game. From the start, though, his favorite game was basketball. "I always had a basketball in my hands as a kid," he recalled. "I was always dribbling and trying new things. Then I'd try to transfer the things I worked on to the court."

For many years, Paul found that the main obstacle to basketball success was his small size. He was only about five feet tall when he entered high school. Every night before bed, he would kneel down and ask God to make him taller. Finally, after an eight-inch growth spurt during his junior year, Paul reached his adult height of six feet. "I've always been vertically challenged. I never grew at all until my junior year of high school. If you call this growing," he laughed. "I knew God wasn't going to get carried away and make me seven feet, two inches. He just gave me enough to get by."

EDUCATION

Paul attended West Forsyth High School near his home in Lewisville. He was a popular student who was elected president of his sophomore, junior, and senior classes. He was an active member of several school clubs and committees, and he served as the school's homecoming king. Since his parents insisted that he maintain at least a 3.0 grade point average if he wanted to play sports, Paul also made the honor roll.

Partly due to his small stature, Paul did not make the varsity basketball team at West Forsyth until his junior year in 2001-02. Still, the young player's dedication to the game impressed the varsity coaching staff. "I played on the junior varsity during my freshman and sophomore years, so I would practice with my team, then when we got done, I would go practice with my older brother's team, the varsity," Paul recalled. "Then I'd go home, eat dinner, then go to the YMCA and play there. I didn't really look at it like I was training or working out with certain guys; I was just playing ball."

Paul's hard work paid off during his junior season, when he became the starting point guard for the West Forsyth Titans varsity basketball team. He averaged an impressive 25 points, 5.3 assists, and 4.4 steals per game to lead his team to a 26-4 won-loss record and the semifinals of the state tournament. The following season went even better for Paul. As a senior in 2002-03, he tallied 30.8 points and 8.0 assists per game and led the Titans to a 27-3 record. Unfortunately, the team was knocked out in the regional finals of the state tournament. Paul's amazing senior season earned him several honors and awards. He was named Mr. Basketball for North Carolina, for instance, as well as a High School All-American.

Honoring His Grandfather

Paul's performance on the basketball court attracted the attention of a number of the top college basketball programs in the country. A week before the start of his senior season, Paul formally accepted a full scholarship to play basketball at his hometown college, Wake Forest University in Winston-Salem. He signed a national letter of intent on November 14, 2002, during a ceremony at his high school that was attended by many family members and friends.

The very next day, Paul's family was rocked by tragedy. His beloved grandfather, Nathaniel Jones, was murdered. Jones had returned home from working at the gas station to find four teenagers robbing his house. The burglars stole his wallet and beat him to death. He was 61 years old.

Paul attended his grandfather's funeral on the day before the first game of his senior high school basketball season. After the service, the grief-stricken teen questioned whether he would be able to join his teammates on the court the next day. Since Jones had always been one of Paul's biggest supporters, though, several family members encouraged him to play in the game. An aunt suggested that Paul find some way to honor his grandfather during the contest.

Inspired, Paul decided that he would try to score 61 points—one for every year of his grandfather's life. He was not sure whether he was capable of the feat (his previous career high was 39 points), so he did not tell anyone about his plan. Once the game got underway, though, it did not take long for his teammates and fans to sense that something special was happening. After scoring 32 points in the first half, Paul continued to scorch the nets in the second half. He hit a lay-up with two minutes remaining in the game to bring his total to 61. He was fouled on the play, but he intentionally missed the resulting free throw. Even though the state high school record of 67 points was within his reach, Paul then took himself out of the game and collapsed in tears on the bench. His remarkable achievement received mention in several national magazines and newspapers.

> *"I played on the junior varsity during my freshman and sophomore years, so I would practice with my team, then when we got done, I would go practice with my older brother's team, the varsity," Paul recalled. "Then I'd go home, eat dinner, then go to the YMCA and play there. I didn't really look at it like I was training or working out with certain guys; I was just playing ball."*

Playing for Wake Forest

Paul graduated from West Forsyth in the spring of 2003. That fall he entered Wake Forest, where he majored in communications and earned a spot on the dean's list. He also became the star point guard on the Demon Deacons basketball team. As a freshman, he averaged 14.8 points per game and led the team in a number of statistical categories, including assists (with 183), steals (84), three-point field goal percentage (.465), and free-throw percentage (.843). His strong performance helped him win the 2003-04 Atlantic Coast Conference (ACC) Rookie of the Year Award and the National Freshman of the Year Award. Wake Forest posted a 21-9 record that year and earned a coveted invitation to the season-ending National Collegiate Athletic Association (NCAA) tournament. Paul raised his scoring average to 21 points in the tournament, but the Demon Deacons lost to St. Joseph's in the third round.

Playing for the Wake Forest Demon Deacons,
Paul hustles to the basket in this game against Duke.

During his sophomore season in 2004-05, Paul emerged as one of the top point guards in the country. He averaged 15.3 points, 6.6 assists, and 2.4 steals per game to lead the Demon Deacons to a 27-6 record. Once again, however, the season ended in a disappointing fashion when Wake Forest lost to West Virginia in the second round of the NCAA tournament. Paul's many post-season honors included being named a consensus first-team All-American. He decided to leave Wake Forest without completing his degree in order to make himself eligible for the 2005 National Basketball Association (NBA) draft.

CAREER HIGHLIGHTS

NBA—The New Orleans Hornets

Paul was selected in the first round of the 2005 draft, with the fourth over-all pick, by the New Orleans Hornets. The Hornets had entered the NBA in 1988 as an expansion team based in Charlotte, North Carolina. The franchise relocated to New Orleans, Louisiana, in 2002. The year before Paul joined the team, the Hornets had struggled to an 18-64 record in the NBA's tough Western Conference.

Despite the addition of a promising young point guard, few people expect-ed the Hornets to do well in 2005-06. Prospects for the season looked even more bleak when Hurricane Katrina roared through the Gulf of Mexico and struck New Orleans in August 2005. The storm caused severe flooding that devastated the city. The Hornets' home stadium suffered serious dam-age, so the team was forced to play most of its home games that year in Oklahoma City, Oklahoma.

Paul and the Hornets overcame this disruption, however, and performed far better than expected. They finished the season with a respectable 38-44 record, more than doubling the previous year's win total. Paul averaged 16.1 points, 7.8 assists, and 2.24 steals per game in his professional debut. He led all rookies in those categories and easily won the NBA Rookie of the Year Award. In addition, his 175 total steals ranked first in the entire league.

In an effort to build a stronger supporting cast for Paul, New Orleans made a number of changes to its roster prior to the 2006-07 season. The Hornets signed free-agent guard Jannero Pargo, acquired small forward Peja Sto-jakovic from the Indiana Pacers, and traded with the Chicago Bulls for cen-ter Tyson Chandler. Unfortunately, it turned out to be a frustrating year for Paul and his teammates. Paul suffered a series of injuries to his foot, ankle, and thumb that kept him out of action for a total of 18 games. "It's been tough," he noted. "It seems like when you come back from one [injury],

Paul in action in 2008, as the team drove toward the playoffs.

another one comes up. But that's how this league is." The absence of their star player proved too much for the Hornets to overcome. Still playing most of their home games in Oklahoma City, they posted a 39-43 record and failed to make the playoffs.

Paul still averaged 17.3 points, 4.4 rebounds, 8.9 assists, and 1.84 steals per game during his second NBA season. In spite of his nagging injuries, he led the Hornets in assists, steals, and total points, and he ranked fourth in the league in assists per game. After the season ended, Paul underwent surgery to repair a stress reaction in his left foot.

Making the NBA Playoffs

With repairs to their stadium completed, the Hornets moved back to New Orleans prior to the start of the 2007-08 season. The team had attracted so many fans in Oklahoma City, however, that the NBA decided to award the city its own franchise. The former Seattle Supersonics announced plans to move there in 2008-09 and become the Oklahoma City Thunder.

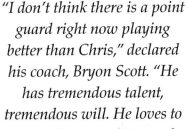

"I don't think there is a point guard right now playing better than Chris," declared his coach, Bryon Scott. "He has tremendous talent, tremendous will. He loves to be out there, winning and doing whatever it takes to knock down an opponent."

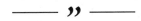

The Hornets' return home helped propel the team to a great start in Paul's third NBA season. New Orleans led the Western Conference with a 29-12 record at the halfway point in the season. As a result, the team's head coach, Byron Scott, was named coach of the Western Conference All-Star Team. The roster included two of his own players, Paul and power forward David West. Paul contributed 16 points, 4 steals, and a game-high 14 assists, but his team lost to the Eastern Conference All-Stars by a score of 134-128. He still enjoyed playing in the All-Star Game, which he described as "totally different from anything I've ever experienced, because this is one of the biggest stages, if not the biggest, as an NBA player."

The Hornets stayed healthy and continued to play well for the remainder of the 2007-08 season. To the surprise of many observers, New Orleans posted the best record in franchise history at 56-26, won the Southwest Division title, and earned the second seed in the Western Conference for the playoffs. "CP [Chris Paul] and I always talked about closing the gap with the best teams in the West," said teammate David West. "We knew if we could stay healthy and stay together, we could do it, and it looks like we've done it. Just maybe a little quicker than we thought."

Paul led the Hornets in scoring, averaging a career-high 21.1 points per game. He also led the entire NBA in assists (with an average of 11.6 per game) and steals (2.7 per game). He thus became the first player to lead the league in both of those categories since Utah Jazz point guard John Stockton did it in 1991-92. Taking note of his individual performance as well as his impact on his team, many people argued that Paul deserved to be named the NBA's Most Valuable Player (MVP). "Chris has his team near the top in the toughest division. He's the best player on our team. He's the floor general, making everyone better," teammate Tyson Chandler explained. "Man, I don't know what an MVP is if it isn't that guy." In the end, however, Paul finished second in the regular-season MVP voting to Los Angeles Lakers star Kobe Bryant.

As the 2007-08 playoffs got underway, the Hornets smoked the Dallas Mavericks in the first round, winning the best-of-seven series four games to one. New Orleans then moved on to face the defending NBA champion San Antonio Spurs in the second round. Paul practically won the first two games in the series himself by scoring a total of 67 points and dishing out 27 assists. "I don't think there is a point guard right now playing better than Chris," declared Coach Scott. "He has tremendous talent, tremendous will. He loves to be out there, winning and doing whatever it takes to knock down an opponent."

Despite Paul's valiant effort, the young Hornets soon relinquished their 2-0 lead and ended up losing the series to the veteran Spurs 4-3. Paul averaged an impressive 24.1 points, 4.9 rebounds, 11.3 assists, and 2.3 steals per game during the playoffs. Afterward, he promised that his team would compete for the NBA title in 2008-09. "We have the tools. We have the talent. We have the personnel," he stated. "We have what it takes."

Winning an Olympic Gold Medal

During the summer of 2008, Paul traveled to Beijing, China, to compete in the Olympic Games as a member of the U.S. Men's National Basketball Team. He had represented the United States in international competition once before, winning a bronze medal at the 2006 World Championships in Japan. Paul was unable to play for the National Team during the summer of 2007, however, because he was recovering from surgery. He was thrilled to have an opportunity to play in the Olympics. "It is the ultimate honor to represent your country," he noted. "I am so proud to be playing for Team USA."

Paul joined a powerful American squad made up of such NBA stars as Kobe Bryant, Jason Kidd, Carmelo Anthony, LeBron James, Dwyane Wade, and Deron Williams. He and his teammates were determined to set their egos aside in order to return home with the gold medal. "We all are just trying to come together and do whatever we need to do to win this gold

In the gold medal game of the 2008 Olympics, Paul and his teammates faced Spain. Team USA took home the gold medal for the first time since 2000.

medal," he stated. "It's not about who plays the most minutes, who gets the most shots. It's about the USA winning at the end."

During the Olympic tournament, Paul led Team USA in assists with 4.1 per game. He also contributed 8.0 points and 3.6 rebounds per contest. After trouncing their opponents in the early rounds, the American squad faced Spain in the gold-medal match. It was a hard-fought contest, but Paul and his teammates prevailed by a score of 118-107. They thus claimed the first gold medal for the United States in men's basketball since the 2000 Games. "The gold medal is one of the highest achievements in my basketball career to date," Paul said afterward. "This was the first time in my life that I've really been a champion. I've always been on winning teams. But to actually be a champion? It has given me something to strive for in the NBA."

Joining the Ranks of Great Players

Prior to the start of the 2008-09 NBA season, Paul signed a three-year contract extension with the Hornets worth an estimated $68 million. The new contract reflected his impact on the team, as well as his popularity with fans in New Orleans. "We are honored to have [him] as the face and future of our franchise," said Hornets owner George Shinn. "The difference between a good player and a great player is character. I think without a doubt Chris Paul has character plus."

As he entered his fourth year in the league, Paul seemed poised to join the ranks of the greatest point guards in NBA history. "When you talk about great point guards in this league that have all had a very big impact on the game, you've got to talk about Magic [Johnson] and Zeke [Isiah Thomas] and [John] Stockton and guys like that," said Byron Scott. "When you start talking about those guys, he's in that sentence somewhere."

> *Paul enjoys being a role model for kids and takes the responsibility very seriously. "It means a lot," he said. "Every time I look at kids, I see myself at that age, knowing I would have loved someone like an NBA player talking to me and letting me know what he did to get there."*

HOME AND FAMILY

Chris Paul, who is single, shares a home in New Orleans with his brother.

HOBBIES AND OTHER INTERESTS

When he is not playing basketball, Paul enjoys watching football (especially the Dallas Cowboys), mountain biking, and listening to music. His favorite hobby, however, is bowling. "My dad used to bowl in leagues all the time," he recalled. "We used to go up there with him. It was a fun family event. Then, when I got to college, I really got into it. My parents bought me my own bowling ball that looks like the old ABA [American Basketball Association] three-color basketball."

Paul sometimes goes bowling twice a day with his brother. His bowling scores average between 180 and 190, and he once tallied a high game of 256. Paul serves as an official spokesman for the U.S. Bowling Congress (USBC). He also hosts an annual charity bowling tournament in Winston-Salem. The 2008 event featured NBA stars LeBron James, Dwyane Wade, and Dwight Howard, as well as professional bowling stars Jason Couch, Chris Barnes, Tommy Jones, and Doug Kent.

Paul also contributes his time and money to a variety of other charitable causes. Shortly after joining the NBA in 2005, for example, he established a foundation to sponsor projects in the Winston-Salem community. Paul also joined forces with other NBA stars to help Habitat for Humanity build homes in areas of New Orleans that were damaged by flooding from Hurricane Katrina. Finally, Paul makes frequent appearances at schools and basketball camps to connect with his young fans. He enjoys being a role model for kids and takes the responsibility very seriously. "It means a lot," he said. "Every time I look at kids, I see myself at that age, knowing I would have loved someone like an NBA player talking to me and letting me know what he did to get there."

Bowling is Paul's favorite hobby.

HONORS AND AWARDS

Mr. Basketball for North Carolina (*Charlotte Observer*): 2003

High School Basketball All-American (McDonald's, *Parade*): 2003

NCAA Men's Basketball Freshman of the Year (*College Insider, Sporting News, Basketball Times*): 2003-04

NCAA Basketball All-American: 2004-05

NBA Rookie of the Year: 2005-06

NBA Community Assist Award: 2006

NBA Western Conference All-Star: 2007-08

Olympic Games, Men's Basketball: 2008, gold medal

FURTHER READING

Periodicals

Atlanta Journal and Constitution, Feb. 27, 2005, p.D1

New York Times, Apr. 8, 2006, p.D1; Apr. 27, 2008, p.L5

Sports Illustrated, Feb. 28, 2005, p.54; Feb. 13, 2006, p.66; Dec. 17, 2007, p.50; Feb. 18, 2008, p.32
Sports Illustrated for Kids, Mar. 2005, p.46; May 2006, p.T4; Apr. 2008, p.20; Nov. 2008, p.28
St. Petersburg Times, Mar. 20, 2004, p.C1
USA Today, Mar. 22, 2007, p.C12; Apr. 11, 2007, p.C8; Feb. 14, 2008, p.E1
Washington Post, Jan. 29, 2004, p.D1

Online Articles

http://sports.espn.go.com/espnmag
    (ESPN. "How Do You Know ... Who's Better?" Nov. 3, 2008)
http://www.nba.com/hornets/news
    (NBA, "Ask Chris Paul: 2008 Offseason," Parts 1-3, 2008)

ADDRESS

Chris Paul
New Orleans Hornets
1250 Poydras Street, Floor 19
New Orleans, LA 70113

WORLD WIDE WEB SITES

http://www.chrispaul3.com
http://www.nba.com/hornets
http://www.nbcolympics.com/athletes

Rachael Ray 1968-

American Professional Cook
Host of Television Cooking Shows and Cookbook
Author

BIRTH

Rachael Domenica Ray was born on August 25, 1968, in Glens
Falls, New York. Her mother, Elsa Providenzia Scuderi, worked
as a restaurant manager. Her father, James Claude Ray,
worked in the food-service industry for some years, and later
as a marketing director for a book publisher. She has a sister,
Maria, who is nine years older, and a brother, Emmanuel, who
is six years younger.

YOUTH

Ray came from a background with a rich heritage in food. Her father was brought up in the French region of Louisiana, where cooking is a key part of the culture. Her mother came from an Italian family where cooking was also very important, both in the home and as a business—the extended family owned several restaurants. Ray was still a baby when her family moved from upstate New York to Cape Cod, in Massachusetts. They lived there for some years. Her parents divorced when she was 12 years old, and after that her mother took the children and moved back up to the Adirondack region of New York, where Ray had been born.

> ——— " ———
>
> *"My grandfather lived with us and was my caretaker, so I liked everything that old Italian men liked," Ray remembered. "I liked sardines and squid and eating calamari with your fingers and anything with anchovies, anything with garlic and oil. I still eat much the same way today. I was not a very popular girl when I opened my lunch sack at the lunchroom."*
>
> ——— " ———

Ray's mother did not like to leave her children in day care. Instead, from the time they were very young, she took them along to work with her at the family's restaurants. Everyone was expected to pitch in and help, whether they were paid for it or not. Ray grew up waiting tables, washing dishes, and preparing food. The family believed that the children would learn by doing. "Nobody says, 'Here's how you peel a potato'—they just say, 'Rachael, peel a potato,'" she recalled. "My first memory in life is grilling my thumb to the griddle in our restaurant on Cape Cod."

As a child, Ray enjoyed foods that many children wouldn't touch. "My grandfather lived with us and was my caretaker, so I liked everything that old Italian men liked," she remembered. "I liked sardines and squid and eating calamari with your fingers and anything with anchovies, anything with garlic and oil. I still eat much the same way today. I was not a very popular girl when I opened my lunch sack at the lunchroom."

EDUCATION

Ray graduated from Lake George High School in Lake George, New York. She attended Pace University in New York, but did not graduate.

FIRST JOBS

After graduating from high school and attending Pace University for a while, Ray decided to move to New York City. She spent two years working at Macy's Marketplace, staffing the candy counter and managing the fresh-food department. Within a few years, she had moved on to be the store manager and buyer at Agata & Valentina, a gourmet market in the heart of the city. She enjoyed her job, but she decided to leave the city. In 1997, she was violently attacked and robbed at her own apartment building twice, in a matter of just two weeks. She decided to head for a safer location and moved back to the Lake George area, where she managed pubs and restaurants for a while. Eventually, she took a position as a food buyer and chef at Cowan & Lobel, a gourmet market in Albany, New York, the state capital.

Good Meals in Half an Hour

While working at Cowan & Lobel, Ray noticed that prepared foods sold very well, but simple, whole ingredients did not. She asked customers some questions and learned that many people felt they didn't have enough time to cook, even if they enjoyed being in the kitchen and were interested in eating well. Ray set out to prove that they could indeed make themselves delicious, healthful dinners even if time was short. She began to give a series of cooking classes to show how to put together a great meal in 30 minutes. In addition, she bundled together packages of the ingredients she used, to make shopping that much easier for the customers.

The classes were a great success, and they attracted people from all walks of life. In fact, they became so popular that in 1998, Ray was asked by WRGB, an Albany-area television station, to start doing a weekly segment on their news broadcast featuring some of her 30-minute meals. Her television segment was nominated for two regional Emmy Awards that year. The success of her "30-Minute" concept continued to expand the following year, when she published a cookbook titled *30-Minute Meals*. In 2001, she published two more cookbooks, *Comfort Foods* and *Veggie Meals*.

CAREER HIGHLIGHTS

Star of the Food Network

Ray made her first national television appearance in 2001. She was asked to appear on the "Today" show, a big-budget morning program on the NBC network. In a segment with the show's weatherman, Al Roker, she made some hearty winter soups and shared tips about using Thanksgiving leftovers. Roker remembered being very impressed with her and later

Ray's first cookbook, 30-Minute Meals, *led to her TV show of the same name and launched her successful cooking career.*

said: "She is unabashedly who she is and makes no apologies, which is what people like about her. She's real…. You see her on camera, and she just pops."

The day after her appearance on "Today," Ray was approached by the Food Network, a cable television company. She was offered a $360,000 contract to work with the network on a variety of projects. Her program "30-Minute Meals" premiered soon after, and it was an immediate success. The show was based on the same concept that she had been pushing since working at the Cowan & Lobel store: that anyone can cook a healthful, delicious meal in about a half an hour. In her quest to make things simple, she didn't hesitate to use shortcuts, such as ready-made salads in a bag, sauce from a jar, or items from the frozen-food section.

> *Ray has readily admitted her own faults: "I'm not a chef, I don't bake, I am loud, I am goofy, and after a while, my voice is annoying."*

The concept was a good one, but a big part of the show's success was Ray's personality. Her delivery was friendly, upbeat, and casual. Unlike some television chefs, she didn't prepare fancy dishes or use complicated methods. Her consistent message was that you don't have to know much about cooking in order to create a good meal. She readily admitted her own faults and has said of herself: "I'm not a chef, I don't bake, I am loud, I am goofy, and after a while, my voice is annoying." She often dropped things on the set or got her lines wrong. She has set not only a loaf of bread on fire, but also her hair. All her quirks and goofs just seemed to boost her appeal, however.

In 2002, while still going strong with "30-Minute Meals," Ray was given a second program on the Food Network. On "$40 a Day," she traveled around the United States and Europe, sampling various restaurants where good meals can be purchased on a budget. In 2004, the Food Network decided to capitalize on her winning personality by moving her beyond the confines of a simple cooking or restaurant-review show. "Inside Dish with Rachael Ray" featured Ray hanging out with various celebrities. They might be in the stars' homes, at their favorite restaurants, or chatting casually while they cooked up some tasty food together. Like "30-Minute Meals" and "$40 a Day," "Inside Dish with Rachael Ray" was a success. In August, 2005, the Food Network launched yet another program, "Rachael Ray's Tasty Travels." This was something like her "$40 a Day" show, but aimed at travelers who were willing and able to spend more money. The

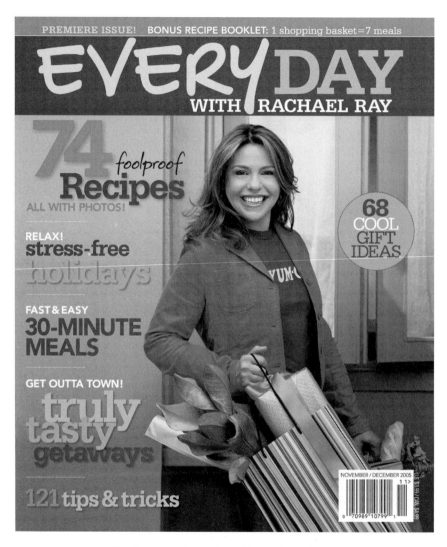

PREMIERE ISSUE!   BONUS RECIPE BOOKLET: 1 shopping basket=7 meals

EVERYDAY
WITH RACHAEL RAY

74 *foolproof* **Recipes**
ALL WITH PHOTOS!

RELAX!
stress-free holidays

FAST & EASY
30-MINUTE MEALS

GET OUTTA TOWN!
truly tasty getaways

121 tips & tricks

68 COOL GIFT IDEAS

NOVEMBER / DECEMBER 2005

*Ray's success has allowed her to branch out
into other areas, including producing a magazine.*

show's exotic locations led to some mishaps, according to Ray: "I've almost drowned on 'Tasty Travels' many times; falling off surfboards, getting caught in undercurrents, deep-sea diving."

Expanding Empire

By 2004, Ray's business ventures were moving far beyond cooking on television. She signed a multi-book contract with Random House, a major publisher. Five of her cookbooks were on the *New York Times* bestseller list during the holiday season that year. Titles from her expanding series of cookbooks sold millions of copies. In fact, *365: No Repeats: A Year of Deliciously Different Dinners* alone sold more than 1.3 million copies. "That was the stupidest idea I ever had," she later said humorously of *365: No Repeats.* "That many recipes nearly killed me."

In 2005, she designed and launched the Gusto-Grip knife collection. Manufactured by Furi, the knives feature a distinctive bright-orange handle. Ray eventually went on to expand her line of signature products to include more cookware, a brand of olive oil, high-quality dog food, and even a microwave oven. She even worked with Epic Records to put out two albums: "How Cool Is That," a selection of Christmas music, and "Too Cool for School," which was aimed at children. Ray didn't perform on either, but chose the selections on each.

Ray's fans could not get enough of her, and the first issue of a new magazine debuted in October 2005, with Ray acting as editor-in-chief. *Every Day with Rachael Ray* was a continuation of her message that good food, and good living, can happen without too much fuss, time, or money. It was illustrated with hundreds of pictures, making it a quick read with lots of visual inspiration. One regular feature was a recipe so simple to make that no written directions were given, only photographed illustrations. The magazine's first issue was eagerly awaited and quickly sold out at many stores on the first day it was available. An additional run of it was printed, and more than a million copies of that first issue were sold.

Multiple television shows, numerous books, product lines, product endorsements, and a monthly magazine led some critics to complain that Ray was overexposed. In response, she said: "I don't put my name on things I don't believe in. I love every page of our magazine. I'm extremely proud of it. I work very hard on each cookbook to make it different." She may have had some detractors, but in 2006, Ray was ranked number 81 on a list of the most powerful celebrities, compiled by the business magazine *Forbes.* She was the top chef on the list. She was also awarded a daytime Emmy Award for her "30-Minute Meals" program that year.

National Talk Show Host

Ray's appeal to TV audiences was noticed by Oprah Winfrey, another woman who had created a business empire based on her strong, winning personality. Winfrey rose to fame as a talk-show host but eventually became one of the most powerful women in the entertainment industry. Taking Ray under her wing, Winfrey encouraged the idea of a nationally syndicated, hour-long talk show featuring Ray. With the backing of Winfrey's production company, Harpo Productions, the "Rachael Ray" show debuted on September 18, 2006. By November of that year it was the top-rated syndicated talk show on the air, and it eventually settled into fourth place behind the popular programs "The Oprah Winfrey Show," "Dr. Phil," and "Live with Regis and Kelly."

Filmed in New York, "Rachael Ray" utilizes an elaborate set that gives the feel of a loft-style apartment. There is a kitchen, a game room with Foosball and air hockey, a living room, a patio, even a garage. The idea was for Ray to invite celebrities to relax with her in her "home." During filming, the audience is seated on a special platform in the middle of the set, which rotates to face whatever area of the set is being used. There would be "no crying, no big stuff," she explained. Instead, she would ask them things like "What your nickname was in fourth grade. What do you have in your fridge right this minute. Those fun, stupid party questions." She worked without a writing staff, using no script or teleprompters.

> In creating her new talk show, Ray had definite ideas for the show's tone and content. There would be "no crying, no big stuff," she explained. "I'm the queen of the little stuff. I want it to be really accessible. With a can-do, party feel rather than a talk-show feel. I want to hear real-life solutions to small problems."

During the course of the show Ray might touch on anything, from celebrity visits, to home remedies, to tips for traveling with children, to recipes for dog treats. "I'm the queen of the little stuff. I want it to be really accessible. With a can-do, party feel rather than a talk-show feel. I want to hear real-life solutions to small problems," she said.

Ray also left the set sometimes, as when she visited NASA headquarters to do a segment on 30-minute meals that could be prepared in space. The "Rachael Ray" show was also responsible for some extravagant gifts to people in need. For example, after the devastating hurricane Ike struck the Gulf Coast of the United States, Ray's show funded a special wedding event for 33 couples whose wedding plans were ruined due to the storm. In another instance, a deadly tornado struck Enterprise, Alabama, leaving eight students dead and destroying the high school. After that tragedy, Ray

In 2006, Ray progressed from TV cook to talk show host.

and her crew organized a prom dance for the school's students at a nearby Air Force base.

Sammies and EVOO

One trait that endears Ray to her fans—while annoying her critics—is her use of slang and made-up words. She frequently refers to dishes as "easy-peasey" to make, calls sandwiches "sammies," and has dubbed a thick soup with stew-like qualities a "stoup." She frequently exclaims "Yum-o!" in anticipation of good food, and "Delish!" when eating something she considers delicious. "EVOO," her term for extra-virgin grade olive oil, became so widely used that in 2007, it was added to the *Oxford English Dictionary*, which is considered the leading reference book on the English language.

Like her language, Ray's personality is cheerful and breezy. Yet she is also very hardworking. She usually only gets about five hours of sleep a night, but she thrives on her fast-paced life-style. "I like hard work," she admitted, "Generally speaking, unless it's pouring rain or I'm really, really sick, it freaks me out to be still." Although her schedule is extremely busy, she appreciates everything she has to do, especially when she compares it to some of the strenuous, physical work she has done in her past—such as unloading heavy crates of food into restaurant kitchens or trying to prepare meals for busloads of tourists at resorts. "I come from very hard-working people," she said. "But, more importantly, they really eat life. They're optimistic, fun, outgoing. Everybody in my family has an over-the-top personality. They just like to create and share."

> "It's just a lot of fun to walk down the street and have people stop you and give you a recipe," she acknowledged. "They'll give me travel tips, coupons to go to different restaurants. And people are always looking out for me, too. People stop me in the street and say, 'Hey, can I help you with those bags there, Rach? How far do you have to go?' It's very down-to-earth and homey. It's nice."

For Ray, fame is one more aspect of life to be enjoyed. "It's just a lot of fun to walk down the street and have people stop you and give you a recipe," she acknowledged. "They'll give me travel tips, coupons to go to different restaurants. And people are always looking out for me, too. People stop me in the street and say, 'Hey, can I help you with those bags there, Rach? How far do you have to go?' It's very down-to-earth and homey. It's nice." On the other hand, fame has also given rise to some negative attention, such as anti-Rachael Ray web sites that relentlessly pick apart her every move. Ray shrugs off that kind of criticism, knowing that it is impossible to please everyone.

Looking to the future, Ray has no specific plans, but said: "If you keep your mind open and your spirit open and you're very hardworking, I think life sort of unfolds and presents itself to you. And so far, it's been more fun than anything I could have planned. So, you know, whatever's the next logical thing that comes out of the growth of this thing that's now got a life of its own, I'll just follow the path."

HOME AND FAMILY

Ray is married to John Cusimano, an entertainment lawyer she met at a party in 2001. The two immediately hit it off and began dating. They were married on September 24, 2005, at a five-day wedding party they held at a castle in Montalcino, Italy. They now have homes in New York City and in the Adirondack region of New York state. Ray was glad to have found someone who understood her fast-paced lifestyle. "Some days I am up at 4:00 a.m. and don't leave work until 9:00," she said. "Luckily I married a man who doesn't mind eating dinner at 10:30 every night." After coming home from work, Ray generally likes to just relax, have something to eat, and watch some television—but not her own programs, which she says she never views because she does not want to become self-conscious.

Cusimano plays in a band called The Cringe, and Ray occasionally enjoys going to hear their music at clubs around New York. She doubts she and her husband will have children, for as she put it: "I work too much to be an appropriate parent. I feel like a bad mom to my dog."

FAVORITE FOODS

Listing her favorite foods, Ray said they change with the seasons: "In the fall and winter, I make soups three nights a week, definitely one with beans and greens. I want more steak and pasta in the winter, but in the summer, I'll make salad suppers with all sorts of delicious things in them. I also like sammies (hollowed-out sandwiches) and, once in a while, a big fruit salad with scrambled eggs. Oh, and I am the queen of burgers."

As far as staying fit in a career that has revolved around food, Ray said, "I do some calisthenics at home when I can," but she noted she's not very consistent about exercising. She added: "I try to eat well—I grew up with a Mediterranean diet, so I don't eat a lot of butter and fat. I eat a lot of vegetables and good, fresh-looking food."

HOBBIES AND OTHER INTERESTS

Ray loves animals, and her pit bull-mix dog, Isaboo, is a very familiar figure to her fans. "I make a huge mess in the kitchen. That's why I have a big dog," she joked, referring to Isaboo's enthusiasm for eating food that falls on the floor. The dog has appeared on Ray's television program and in her magazine, both of which have featured articles on tasty foods meant for shared human and animal snacking.

Ray's concern for animals, especially dogs, led her to develop Nutrish, a special brand of dog food. Some of her pet-food products are named after her own beloved dog. Customers can buy Isaboo Booscotti crunchy treats and Isaboo Grill Bites chewy treats. All the proceeds from sales of her pet-food products go to support an animal-rescue program called Rachael's Rescue.

Another charitable cause Ray energetically supports is the Yum-O Organization, a nonprofit foundation created to help children and families improve their relationships with food. Yum-O's mission has three parts: to educate all people about cooking good food for a reasonable amount of

A dog lover, Ray launched a line of pet food, Nutrish.

money; to help feed hungry children in America; and to help young people who want to attend cooking schools by providing scholarships.

"Growing up, I had a very healthy relationship with food and cooking and, throughout my life, I've met people who were positively influenced by lessons learned in the kitchen," Ray explained. "We've created Yum-o! to introduce more kids to cooking, which can have such a meaningful impact on their lives and health. Food definitely brings a smile to my face and so many great memories can be made by spending time together as a family in the kitchen." With Yum-O!, Ray hopes to "get parents and kids cooking healthier breakfasts, lunches, lunchboxes, and dinners and we want to make food fun, fast, and affordable for American families.... The challenge I've heard from parents is that they don't have the time or money to cook healthier. They just don't believe they can make good food fast and that is just not true."

SELECTED CREDITS

Television

"30-Minute Meals," 2002–
"$40 a Day," 2002–
"Inside Dish with Rachael Ray," 2004–
"Rachael Ray's Tasty Travels," 2005–
"Rachael Ray," 2006–

Books

30-Minute Meals, 1999
Veggie Meals, 2001
30-Minute Meals 2, 2003
Cooking Rocks! Rachael Ray's 30-Minute Meals for Kids, 2004
$40 a Day: Best Eats in Town, 2004
Guy Food, 2005
Rachael Ray Express Lane Meals, 2006
Just in Time, 2007
Yum-O! The Family Cookbook, 2008

HONORS AND AWARDS

Daytime Emmy (National Academy of Television Arts and Sciences): 2006, for Outstanding Service Show, for "30-Minute Meal"
Daytime Emmy (National Academy of Television Arts and Sciences): 2008, for Outstanding Talk Show, for "Rachael Ray"

FURTHER READING

Periodicals

Current Biography Yearbook, 2005
Good Housekeeping, Aug. 2006, p.114
Newsweek, Sep.12, 2005, p.72
People, Dec. 5, 2005, p.109; May 14, 2007, p.118
Redbook, Oct. 2006, p.60

Television Week, Jan. 15, 2007, pp.41, 48
Time, Sep. 11, 2006, p.75
USA Today, Sep. 14, 2006, p.D1

ADDRESS

Rachael Ray
Food Network
75 Ninth Avenue
New York, NY 10011

WORLD WIDE WEB SITES

http://www.rachaelray.com
http://www.rachaelrayshow.com
http://www.foodnetwork.com

Emma Roberts 1991-

American Actress
Star of the Television Show "Simply Fabulous" and
the Films *Nancy Drew* and *Hotel for Dogs*

BIRTH

Emma Rose Roberts was born on February 10, 1991, in
Rhinebeck, New York (some sources say Los Angeles, California). Her father is Eric Roberts, an actor, and her mother is
Kelly Cunningham, a producer. Roberts and Cunningham
separated when their daughter was about two months old.
Roberts's father married Eliza Garrett, an actress who had two
children from a previous marriage—a son, Keaton Simons,

and a daughter, Morgan Simons (Emma's step-brother and step-sister). Roberts's mother later married Kelly Nickles, a bassist who formerly played in the band L.A. Guns; they had one daughter, Grace (Emma's half-sister).

YOUTH

Roberts has grown up in a family that is deeply involved in show business. Her grandparents on her father's side, Walter Roberts and Betty Lou Motes, were both known as outstanding acting teachers in Atlanta, Georgia. Their three children, Eric, Julia, and Lisa, all took up acting careers. Emma Roberts's father, Eric, started in show-business when he was just seven years old. By the time his daughter was born, he had been nominated for an Academy Award for his work in the 1985 film *Runaway Train.* Eric's sisters Julia and Lisa also went into acting. Julia Roberts took her career to the top, becoming an Academy Award winner and the highest-paid actress in the world. Lisa Roberts Gillan has not become as famous as her brother and sister, but she has had small parts in many films.

> *Roberts has grown up in a family that is deeply involved in show business, and she decided she was ready to start her own professional acting career when she was nine. "I think it's in my blood," she once said. "All the Robertses want to be in the movie business."*

Emma Roberts had her first exposure to filmmaking when she was only two weeks old. Her father was working on the movie *Final Analysis* when she was born, and she was often taken to the set. Because of her family connections, she had chances to watch some of the top actors in the business at work, even when she was very young. When she was nine, she announced she was ready to start her own professional acting career. "I think it's in my blood. All the Robertses want to be in the movie business," she once said.

Roberts's mother was a little concerned, because she wanted her daughter to have as normal a childhood as possible. That is often difficult for child actors, and it would be even more of a challenge for someone who would attract extra media attention because of her celebrity relatives. Her mother agreed to let her audition for parts, but only under certain conditions. Roberts would have to keep up with her schoolwork, maintain a social life with her friends, continue doing her usual household chores, and attend college when she was old enough. As her mother said, "Life is a long road and she's got to be prepared for it."

EDUCATION

Until the end of seventh grade, Roberts attended the Archer School for Girls, located in the Brentwood area of Los Angeles, California. After seventh grade she left school, but continued her education by home-schooling and studying with tutors. Roberts has an outgoing personality, and it was hard to leave the social life at school. "I miss it a little bit," she said. "I miss seeing my friends every day. But I go to my friends' school for things like dances and football games. So it's not too bad."

FIRST JOBS

Roberts's career got off to a fast start. At her very first audition, she won a part in a major motion picture, *Blow* (2001), starring Johnny Depp and Penelope Cruz. Depp is one of the top stars in the movie industry, but, Roberts said, "I was so young. I didn't understand that I was working with one of the best actors ever until later." *Blow* is based on the true story of George Jung, a drug dealer. Depp and Cruz played Jung and his wife, and Roberts portrayed their daughter, Kristina. Because of the movie's subject matter, she has still never seen the whole movie, only the scenes in which she appeared. She next acted in a quirky, short movie called *BigLove* (2001), which was first shown at the Sundance Film Festival.

After *BigLove*, Roberts had leading roles in a couple of films with animal co-stars. *Grand Champion* (2001) is a story about a farm family and their beloved prize steer, Hokey Pokey. Financial troubles force the family to sell Hokey Pokey, but when the children learn his life is in danger, they set out on a mission to save him. "It was so much fun to do, especially as I got to go to Texas, where I'd never been before and I loved it there," she recalled. "I got to hang out with a lot of other kids, and we all learned so much about cattle and that whole way of life. I mean, I grew up in L.A., so it was a real education."

Roberts took on a very different role in her next project, *Spymate*. In this film, she played the part of a brilliant young inventor. She is kidnapped by people who want to use her knowledge to help them gain control over the world. In *Spymate*, she co-starred with a chimpanzee. Being an animal lover, she enjoyed the unique opportunity to get to know a chimp. "They're really sweet, and it's incredible to see that they're animals and they're working like that," she said.

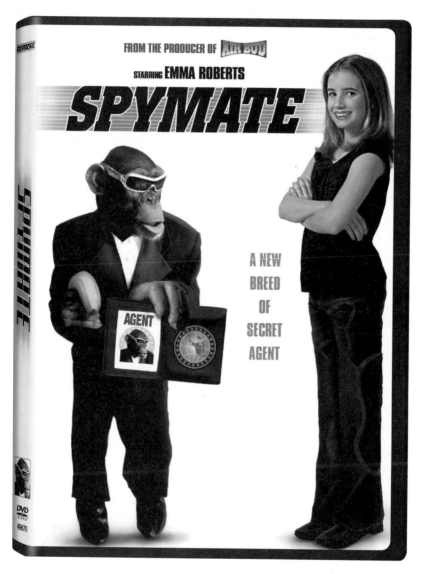

Roberts's success in Spymate,
one of her early movies, helped her win the role in "Unfabulous."

CAREER HIGHLIGHTS

"Unfabulous"

Following her success in *Spymate,* Roberts was asked to meet with executives from the Nickelodeon television network to discuss a new TV series.

Before long, 12-year-old Roberts was cast as Addie Singer, the lead in a new comedy called "Unfabulous." Her co-stars included Molly Hagan as Addie's mother, Sue; Markus Flanagan as her dad, Jeff; Tadhg Kelly as her brother, Ben; Jordan Calloway as her best male friend, Zach, and Malese Jow as her best girlfriend, Geena. Roberts enjoyed being on the set with lots of other people her own age, and her co-stars found her nice to be around. "Emma is always full of energy. She's got a charisma that makes everyone around her want to get up and do something fun," said Tadhg Kelly. "She can make even the longest scenes fly by with her upbeat personality and sense of humor."

> "Like some girls, she wants to fit in," Roberts said about her character, Addie, on "Unfabulous." "She wants to throw the best party, but at the same time she's happy with who she is. She's glad that she's getting through middle school and getting through life."

"Unfabulous" centers on Addie, a middle-school student going through all the frustrations and insecurities common to kids her age: homework, having a crush on someone, worrying about being popular at school. "Like some girls, she wants to fit in. She wants to throw the best party, but at the same time she's happy with who she is," Roberts said. "She's glad that she's getting through middle school and getting through life." One way she copes with daily life is by writing and singing songs about the things she is experiencing, just as some people express themselves by writing in a diary. These songs are often silly or downright funny. They are all written by Jill Sobule, but Roberts really did sing and play the guitar on the program—luckily she had taken guitar lessons since she was nine years old. "Addie's actually really good at playing the guitar, but singing? She's not supposed to be the best," she acknowledged. In 2005, an album featuring music from the showwas released, titled *Unfabulous and More: Emma Roberts.*

The first episode of "Unfabulous" aired on September 12, 2004, during the Sunday night programming block that included the shows "Romeo," "Drake and Josh," and "Ned's Declassified School Survival Guide." The show was an immediate hit with young viewers. Three seasons of "Unfabulous" were produced, with one finale episode shown in the fourth season. When filming ended in 2007, it was an emotional experience. "Nobody was going to cry, and then when they said, 'That's a wrap,' I started getting teary-eyed. Everyone was very sad." Roberts recalled.

Roberts as Addie in "Unfabulous."

Aquamarine

The success of "Unfabulous" kicked Roberts's career into high gear. In 2006, she played a lead role in the comic movie *Aquamarine,* co-starring with the singer Joanna "JoJo" Levesque and the actress Sara Paxton. Roberts played Claire, a shy girl whose parents have both died. Claire is "totally opposite of me," she said. "She's really shy and really afraid of everything and doesn't want to take any chances. But it's fun to play a character that's not like yourself." JoJo played Claire's best friend, Hailey. Together the girls make an amazing discovery: a mermaid has ended up in the pool at their beach club. The mermaid, Aquamarine (played by Paxton), is curious about how humans live. She especially wants to find out about the human emotion called "love." Aquamarine promises Claire and Hailey that she will grant them a wish if they will help her to find love.

Aquamarine was filmed in Australia. Traveling there and getting to hang out with her two costars was lots of fun for Roberts, especially because she had already been a fan of JoJo's music. When the girls weren't on the set working, they were able to spend time biking, swimming, and enjoying themselves at the beach. They had so much fun together that it was sometimes hard to get in the right mood to film some of the dramatic scenes about the characters' problems. "We all had a great time laughing so it was hard to get in the mode of sadness. I also just find it really embarrassing!" Roberts commented.

Nancy Drew

Roberts's next film was a movie adaptation of the *Nancy Drew* mystery books. The book series, popular with young readers since the 1930s, features a title character who is prepared for any situation—from riding a circus horse to translating ancient manuscripts. The daughter of a well-to-do lawyer, Nancy is also an amateur detective who never fails to solve the case. Although the series has been updated periodically to reflect modern innovations, the 2007 movie *Nancy Drew* took a unique twist. It opens in black-and-white, and by the look of the clothing and furniture, Nancy and her father could be living in the 1950s.

Before long, however, Nancy's father takes a job in Los Angeles, and Nancy is shown transferring to a very modern Hollywood High School, where all the students are hooked into 21st century technology and fashion. Nancy's sense of style and ethics are greatly at odds with what she finds at Hollywood High, but she stays true to herself. By the end of the movie, her styles have become trendsetting at the school. Meanwhile, Nancy solves an old mystery involving a movie star who once lived in the

As Nancy Drew, Roberts looks a little out of place in a modern classroom.

house she and her father have rented. The movie combined elements of comedy, mystery, adventure, and romance.

Roberts enjoyed playing the famous character. "She's very kind, very genuine, very sweet," she said. "I think she just really teaches you it's OK for girls to be smart and well-mannered. You don't have to play stupid, and it's cool to be independent and take charge." The actress hadn't read any of the *Nancy Drew* books before she got the part, but she was given lots of copies of them after she was associated with the role. She didn't want to read too many before making the movie, however, preferring to stick to the character as it was written in the script.

Recent Projects

With starring roles in major movies to her credit, and good reviews for her performances in them as well, Roberts could now pick and choose among many projects. In 2008, she took a role in an independent film, *Lymelife,* about the pressures of adolescence and life in the well-to-do suburbs of New York City. After that, she appeared in two films with wide appeal to young audiences: *Wild Child* and *Hotel for Dogs.*

In the 2008 movie *Wild Child,* Roberts played Poppy, a spoiled, bratty rich girl from Malibu, California, whose behavior worsens after the death of her mother. Aiden Quinn played Poppy's father, who has given his daughter very little discipline since his wife died. In his youth, he was responsible for some wild pranks, and Poppy follows in his footsteps. At last she gets in so much trouble that her father decides to send her to a very strict British boarding school, run by the headmistress Mrs. Kingsley, played by Natasha Richardson.

Arriving in England, Poppy is horrified to find that the school doesn't allow fashionable clothes, iPods, cell phones, and all the other luxuries she depends on. Even worse, she finds herself at the bottom of the social order, whereas at home, she was always popular. The ruling clique of girls, led by a girl named Harriet, particularly scorn her because she is American. Eventually, Poppy is humbled enough to make friends with her roommates Josie, Kate, Kiki, and Drippy—four girls who are nearly as unpopular as she is. They agree to help her get in so much trouble that she will be expelled. Harriet temporarily spoils Poppy's plans and her newfound friendships, however. In

> *Roberts enjoyed playing Nancy Drew. "She's very kind, very genuine, very sweet," she said. "I think she just really teaches you it's OK for girls to be smart and well-mannered. You don't have to play stupid, and it's cool to be independent and take charge."*

the end, Poppy must make peace with her classmates and learn how to thrive at her new school—with the help of the headmistress's handsome son, played by Alex Pettyfer.

In 2009, Roberts played a lead role in *Hotel for Dogs,* an adaptation of the popular book of the same name by the author Lois Duncan. The movie concerns two siblings who hide stray dogs in an abandoned hotel. Roberts played Andi and Jake T. Austin played Bruce, her younger brother. Andi and Bruce are orphans who were placed in foster care after the death of their parents. They live in a series of foster homes before landing with the Scudders (played by Lisa Kudrow and Kevin Dillon), a couple of middle-aged aspiring rock-n-rollers who don't have much talent. The kids and their dog Friday, who they hide from the Scudders, find an old, abandoned building, the Francis Duke Hotel, where a few stray dogs live. With the help of some kids who work at a nearby pet shot, Andi and Bruce start taking in other stray animals. Bruce is a gifted inventor, and he creates some clever inventions to help care for the animals when he and Andi are not available.

Scenes from Hotel for Dogs.

Hotel for Dogs was called a fun film for kids and their parents, with a strong message about the importance of family. "I thought this film was special," Roberts declared. "While it is about dogs, it is also a movie about family. It has a great message about how family just doesn't have to be those you are related to. It can be those you feel comfortable with."

HOME AND FAMILY

Roberts lives with her mother, her stepfather, and her half-sister Grace. Even though she is a celebrity, her life is, in some ways, just like a typical teenager's. She has to do chores around the house and she must keep up with her schoolwork. She has two cats, Pirate and Coco Chanel. Coco was named after a famous French fashion designer.

MAJOR INFLUENCES

One of the major influences on Roberts's life has been growing up in a family of actors. Yet being asked about her famous relatives is one of her least favorite things about being a celebrity. Referring to her aunt, Julia Roberts, she revealed that while they are very close, they spend time together doing normal activities. "People always ask me if she give me lots of advice, but we really don't talk about movies or the business. We'll cook or talk about fashion, that kind of thing." Overall, she feels that "a well-known relative can get you in the door, but talent and hard work are what counts." As proof of that, she said, "I've gone on maybe a hundred auditions where I've never even been called back."

Roberts is close to her aunt, actress Julia Roberts. "People always ask me if she give me lots of advice, but we really don't talk about movies or the business. We'll cook or talk about fashion, that kind of thing." Overall, she feels that "a well-known relative can get you in the door, but talent and hard work are what counts."

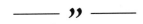

FAVORITE BOOKS AND MUSIC

Roberts enjoys lots of different kinds of music, but some of her favorite recording artists are Usher, Jesse McCartney, Ashlee Simpson, Jessica Simpson, Michelle Branch, JoJo, Eminem, and John Mayer. Her favorite actresses include Reese Witherspoon, Drew Barrymore, Wynona Ryder, and Rachel McAdams. Some of her favorite books are *To Kill a Mockingbird, The Perks of*

Being a Wallflower, My Sister's Keeper, and the "Gossip Girl" series. She reads about one book each week. She is a spokeswoman for Drop Everything and Read (DEAR), a program that sets aside free reading time during the school day. "Kids today have so much technology (computers, Sidekicks, BlackBerrys, etc. which I love by the way!) that I think it is important to encourage them to read and spend quality time with their families."

HOBBIES AND OTHER INTERESTS

One of Roberts's greatest interests is fashion. She has thought about being a fashion designer instead of an actress some day. "I like cute dresses and colorful, comfortable stuff like jeans or a jean skirt and a casual top," she said. Roberts likes to knit, but admits that she doesn't try anything too complicated and has made mostly scarves. She also enjoys being active in sports such as volleyball and tennis, and she loves to cook. Photography is a special interest of hers, one she is considering studying in college.

SELECTED CREDITS

Movies

Blow, 2001
BigLove, 2001 (short)
Grand Champion, 2002
Spymate, 2006
Aquamarine, 2006
Nancy Drew, 2007
Lymelife, 2008
Wild Child, 2008
Hotel for Dogs, 2009

Television

"Unfabulous," 2004-07

Recordings

Unfabulous and More: Emma Roberts, 2005

HONORS AND AWARDS

ShoWest Awards: 2007, Female Star of Tomorrow

FURTHER READING

Books

Brown, Lauren. *Emma Roberts: Simply Fabulous!,* 2007

Periodicals

Girls' Life, Oct.-Nov. 2005, p.44; June-July 2007, p. 44
Kidsworld Magazine, Winter 2007, p.14
Teen Vogue, May 2007, p.138
Times (London), Oct. 6, 2007, p.6
USA Today, Mar. 3, 2006, p.E6; Jan. 7, 2005, p.E4; June 14, 2007, p.D3
Variety, Mar. 6, 2006, p.20

ADDRESS

Emma Roberts
Sweeney Management
8755 Lookout Mountain Avenue
Los Angeles, CA 90046

WORLD WIDE WEB SITES

http://www.emmaroberts.net
http://www.nick.com/shows/unfabulous/index.jhtml
http://nancydrewmovie.warnerbros.com
http://www.wildchildmovie.com
http://www.hotelfordogsmovie.com

Dinara Safina 1986-

Russian Professional Tennis Player
Silver Medal Winner at the 2008 Olympic Games

BIRTH

Dinara Mikhailovna Safina (pronounced *di-NAH-ruh SAF-i-nah*) was born on April 27, 1986, in Moscow, Russia. Her father, Mikhail Alekseyvich Safin, runs the Spartak Tennis Club in Moscow. Her mother, Rauza Islanova, is a tennis coach who has worked with a number of young Russian stars, including Elena Dementieva. Dinara has a brother, fellow professional tennis player Marat Safin, who is six years older.

Safina uses a different form of her last name than the rest of her family, who spell their name "Safin." She spells her last name differently because, in accordance with Russian tradition, she added the feminine ending "a" to the end.

YOUTH AND EDUCATION

Thanks to their parents' professions, Dinara and her brother Marat practically grew up on a tennis court. "I had no choice but to become a tennis player," she conceded, "but I don't mind being a tennis player." With their mother serving as their coach, both children showed talent from an early age.

> *Thanks to their parents' professions, Dinara and her brother Marat practically grew up on a tennis court. "I had no choice but to become a tennis player," she conceded, "but I don't mind being a tennis player."*

When Marat was 16, he turned professional and moved to Spain to further his training. Four years later, he upset the great American champion Pete Sampras to win the 2000 U.S. Open—one of the four major tournaments (along with the Australian Open, French Open, and Wimbledon) that make up the Grand Slam of professional tennis. Following his U.S. Open triumph, Marat was ranked as the number one men's singles player in the world for a time.

Meanwhile, Dinara learned to hit tennis balls at the age of three and began entering junior tournaments at the age of eight. She was 14 when Marat won his first Grand Slam tournament. As a promising young player in her own right, she often found it difficult to be the little sister of a famous champion. "Every time, it's the same thing," she complained. "People want to know what [Marat] is doing and how he is faring. All the time the questions are about him."

Like her brother, Dinara gained a reputation for having a strong serve, hitting powerful ground strokes, and showing emotion on the court. They both had a tendency to argue line calls, for instance, and throw their rackets in frustration. "I think he's an entertainer to watch," she said of Marat. "That's why people love to watch him play, because he always gives some show. I mean, he's real on the court. If he has his emotions, he will not hide them. He will explode."

Dinara claimed that she and her brother inherited their hot tempers from their father, who always hated to lose. "My dad, he's also like a character," she explained. "Even if he plays football [soccer] for fun, when he loses with friends he comes home and he's so angry. And I'm like, 'Pop, it's only a friends match.' But he ... always wants to win."

CAREER HIGHLIGHTS

Turning Pro

Safina turned professional in 2000, just as her brother was reaching the height of his fame. She started out by playing on the International Tennis Federation (ITF) Women's Circuit, which is considered a training ground for the Sony Ericsson Women's Tennis Association (WTA) Tour. She began playing in

Safina won her first victory in a WTA tennis tournament in Poland in 2002, when she was just 16.

professional tennis tournaments, which are organized in rounds of competition. Winning players advance to the next round, while losing players are eliminated. Most tournaments consist of three or four preliminary rounds, followed by quarterfinals (featuring 8 players), semifinals ([4 players), and finals (2 players). The player who wins the final match is the tournament champion and claims the title. Throughout the season, a player plays in many tournaments, and points are totaled for the season.

Scoring in tennis can be confusing. In women's tennis, a player wins a match by defeating her opponent in 2 out of 3 sets. The first player to win 6 games usually wins the set, but if their margin of victory is less than 2 games, the set is decided by a tiebreaker. Shorthand notation is often used to show the score of a tennis match. For example, 6-4, 2-6, 7-6 means that the player in question won the first set by a score of 6 games to 4, lost the next set 2 games to 6, and came back to win the match in a third-set tiebreaker.

When Safina starting playing tennis professionally, she was just 14, so her mother traveled with her and served as her coach. "I do have my mum with me, and that helps a lot as I know I can look to her and have her tell me where I am going right or wrong," Safina acknowledged. "But sometimes one can get tired of being with a person for a full 24 hours at a stretch."

In 2001, Safina showed some promise as a pro. Although she failed to qualify for the WTA Tour, she won one singles and one doubles title on the ITF Circuit that year. She also reached the girls' singles final at Wimbledon as a junior player. By the end of the season, she was ranked 394th among female tennis players around the world.

In 2002, Safina began playing consistently on the WTA Tour. In only her fourth event on the Tour, she claimed her first singles title at Sopot, Poland, beating Henrieta Nagyova of Slovakia 6-3, 4-0 (retired). Safina also continued to compete on the ITF Circuit, winning three singles and two doubles titles. Her strong performance also helped her break into the top 100 in the world rankings. By the time the season drew to a close, she had climbed to number 68.

The 2003 season saw Safina win the second WTA Tour singles title of her career at Palermo, Italy, beating Katarina Srebotnik of Slovenia 6-3, 6-4. She also turned in her best performance at a Grand Slam tournament, advancing to the fourth round at the U.S. Open. Safina ended the season ranked number 54 in the world.

The 2004 season started out well for Safina. During the early part of the year, she beat three players ranked in the top 20 in the world. She also claimed her first WTA Tour doubles title in Beijing, China. Unfortunately, she injured her lower back at Wimbledon and was forced to withdraw from several later tournaments with what turned out to be a lumbar spine stress fracture. Still, Safina managed to rise to number 44 in the world rankings by the end of the year.

Growing Up

By the start of the 2005 season—her sixth as a professional tennis player—some analysts began to wonder whether Safina had already reached the greatest heights of her professional career. After all, she had hovered in the middle of the Top 100 in the world rankings for three straight seasons without showing many signs that she could regularly challenge the sport's reigning stars. But her brother thought that a coaching change might help her. He suggested that it might be time for Safina to end her coaching relationship with her mother, and she decided to follow Marat's advice. "Sometimes he's a little hard, but he wants the best for me," she stated. "He told me I was traveling too much with my mom and when I was play-

Safina reacting after the victory point over Amelia Mauresmo during the 2005 Paris Indoors tournament. She beat Mauresmo 6-4, 2-6, 6-3.

ing I was looking too much at her and waiting for help. Now I'm playing alone, I'm more mature and concentrate more. That's what my mom wanted for me, too."

Safina acknowledged that her relationship with her mother improved once she found a new tennis coach. "It was tough. We saw a lot of each other. We lived together and worked together," she revealed. "She'd get uptight and we'd begin to fight about stupid things, like where I put my phone. It's just like any family when you spend too much time together. It's better now."

Under the guidance of Dutch coach Glen Schaap, Safina resumed her rise through the ranks of women's tennis. She won her third WTA Tour singles title at the Paris Indoors, defeating French star Amelie Mauresmo in the finals by a score of 6-4, 2-6, 6-3. Safina described it as "the best day of my career so far and my biggest victory ever." She took another Tour singles title in Prague, Czech Republic, beating Czech player Zuzana Ondraskova 7-6, 6-3. Safina also reached the semifinals in four other events that year. Her strong performance helped her jump to number 20 in the world rankings.

As it turned out, though, 2005 was an even bigger year for Marat Safin. After struggling with injuries for several seasons, he came back to win a second career Grand Slam title at the Australian Open. In the midst of all the media attention he received, Safin made several critical comments about his younger sister. He told reporters that Safina needed to get in better shape and learn to control her emotions if she wanted to reach the top of women's tennis. "She needs to have a character, and she needs to be a little bit of a grown-up woman," he declared. "With all respect, [when I was her age] I had been number one in the world."

Although Safina was stung by her brother's criticism, she admitted that he had a point.

> *Safina acknowledged that her relationship with her mother improved once she found a new tennis coach. "It was tough. We saw a lot of each other. We lived together and worked together," she revealed. "She'd get uptight and we'd begin to fight about stupid things, like where I put my phone. It's just like any family when you spend too much time together. It's better now."*

"I would behave like a baby and be crying and all this. He hated it. He was always, 'Come on! You have to grow up in your mind,'" she related. "I also knew that I had to be in much better shape to play against top players. I had to be much fitter."

Working Hard

Safina took her brother's words to heart and worked hard to improve her conditioning prior to the start of the 2006 season. Her dedication paid off in several impressive performances. Although she failed to win any titles, Safina defeated four players ranked among the top 10 in the world, reached the semifinals in two events, and made career-best quarterfinal appearances in two Grand Slam tournaments (the French Open and U.S. Open).

Safina's new and improved game was on full display when she stunned Russian star Maria Sharapova in the fourth round of that year's French Open. After trailing her opponent 5 games to 1 in the third set, Safina scored 18 of the last 21 points for an exciting comeback victory, 7-5, 2-6, 7-5. "I think it's unbelievable what I did, just to come back," Safina said afterward. "I took everything in my hands. Before, she was dictating and I had always to run from corner to corner. I said, 'OK, now I'll try to make

Safina beat Martina Hingis to win the
2007 Gold Coast tournament in Australia, 6-3, 3-6, 7-5.

her run.' I started to be more aggressive." Safina ended the 2006 season ranked number 11 in the world in women's singles. She also moved up to number 15 in doubles after winning two titles and reaching the final of the U.S. Open with partner Katarina Srebotnik.

Before the start of the 2007 season, Safina decided to change coaches again. She had trouble getting along with Schaap, and she felt that their conflicts off the court affected her performance on the court. "He would not accept what I would say. He didn't want to hear my opinions," she stated. "I have enough stress on the court playing a match and if I go practice and I'm still fighting with my coach, I don't need this."

Safina credited her new coach, Zeljko Krajan of Croatia, with helping her learn to control her emotions. "I had many coaches, but they could not deal with this," she explained. "He just changed me. I trust him fully." Safina also began working with a new trainer, Dejan Vojnovic of Croatia, who helped her improve her strength, speed, agility, and endurance.

These changes helped Safina claim her fifth career Tour singles title at the 2007 Gold Coast tournament in Australia. Following her victory over

Martina Hingis in the final, 6-3, 3-6, 7-5, Hingis predicted that "Everyone's going to have to watch her." Safina followed that up with another big win—the first Grand Slam victory of her career. She and partner Nathalie Dechy won the 2007 U.S. Open doubles title, beating a team from Chinese Taipei, Yung-Jan Chan and Chia-Jung Chuang, with a score of 6-4, 6-2. By the end of the year Safina was ranked number 15 in the world in women's singles.

On a Roll

The 2008 season began disappointingly for Safina when she lost in the first round of the Australian Open in January. Her struggles continued until May, when she suddenly emerged as one of the hottest players on the Sony Ericsson WTA Tour. The breakthrough began at the German Open in Berlin, when Safina defeated three top 10 players (Justine Henin, Serena Williams, and Elena Dementieva) on her way to winning the sixth Tour singles title of her career, ultimately defeating Dementieva in the finals 3-6, 6-2, 6-2.

Safina's success continued at the French Open in May, where she once again beat three top 10 players (Sharapova, Dementieva, and Svetlana Kuznetsova) to reach her first Grand Slam final as a singles player. Safina demonstrated her newfound physical fitness and mental toughness in each of these triumphs. In the fourth round, for example, she was down 5-3 in the second set against top-seeded Sharapova, facing her opponent's serve at match point. Safina escaped elimination with a backhand winner up the line, then got aggressive and won the match 6-7, 7-6, 6-2. In the quarterfinals against Dementieva, meanwhile, Safina rallied from a 5-2 deficit in the second set to win 4-6, 7-6, 6-0.

After defeating Kuznetsova in the semifinals, Safina had a chance to become part of the only brother-sister combination to both win Grand Slam titles during the Open era of professional tennis (since 1968). She tried to remain focused as she prepared for her first appearance in a major singles final. "I have to do the things that I know to do and try to avoid thinking as much as I can about 'this is the final,'" she noted. "It's still the same court and still the same ball. It's just how I take it in my mind." Unfortunately for Safina, she lost in the final to Ana Ivanovic, snapping her winning streak at 12 matches.

Winning an Olympic Medal

In May, while Safina was in the middle of her winning streak, Russia announced the members of its national tennis team that would compete in the 2008 Olympic Games in Beijing, China. Since several Russian players were ahead of her in the world rankings at that time, Safina did not make the team. After the French Open, however, Russian team member Anna Chakvetadze decided not to compete in the Games. Based on her strong performance in recent tournaments, Safina was selected to replace her.

As the Olympics approached, Safina continued playing on the WTA Tour, and her hot streak continued also. Although she was knocked out in the third round of Wimbledon in June, she won two tournaments in a row in July. Her seventh career title on the WTA Tour came at the East West Bank Classic in Los Angeles, where she beat Flavia Pennetta of Italy 6-4, 6-2. She quickly followed that up with her eighth WTA title at the Rogers Cup in Montreal, Canada, beating Dominika Cibulkova of Slovakia 6-2, 6-1. Going into the Olympic Games, Safina had reached the finals in five out of six tournaments in a row and attained a career-high number 6 in the world rankings.

> *"For some people I will always just be [Marat's] younger sister. But we have completely different lives. Whatever I have achieved and will achieve, I have done by myself," she noted. "I always wanted to be myself, and now finally the results are coming, and people can know me as Dinara Safina."*

Safina flew directly from Montreal to Beijing and did not even have a day off before she began playing in the Olympic tournament. Despite struggling with fatigue, she defeated hometown favorite Li Na of China in the quarterfinals and top-ranked Jelena Jankovic in the semifinals to face Dementieva in the gold medal match. Safina did her best, but she had to settle for the silver medal. "I'm not a machine, I'm a human being," she said afterward of the grueling schedule. "Of course it's sad that it's not the gold medal, but it doesn't matter given what I've done, not many girls can do it."

Reaching for the Top

Immediately after the Olympic Games ended, Safina traveled to America to compete in the U.S. Open. If she managed to capture her first Grand Slam singles title, she stood to win a $1 million bonus and claim the world number one ranking. Safina fought hard in the tournament and made it all the way to the semifinals before losing to Serena Williams.

*After winning the silver medal at the 2008 Olympics, Safina (left)
is shown here with fellow medalists Elena Dementieva (gold, center)
and Vera Zvonareva (bronze, right).*

Safina came back strong to win the next tournament she entered, the Pan
Pacific Open in Tokyo, Japan, beating fellow Russian Svetlana Kuznetsova
6-1, 6-3. She thus claimed the ninth WTA Tour title of her career and
moved up to the number 2 position in the world rankings. After the match,
Kuznetsova was full of praise for Safina's game. "She works very hard and
she has lots of energy, and I think she has much more confidence now,"
she said. "She has been one of the strongest players on the tour in the second half of the season."

From the time her hot streak started at Berlin in May, Safina posted an
amazing match record of 37 wins and 5 losses. She raised her career win-
loss record to 281-130 and boosted her career earnings to $5.3 million in
prize money. Although Safina ended her spectacular 2008 season without
winning a Grand Slam singles title, she feels confident that she will one
day match her brother's achievement. "I think it's going to be the dream of
our family," she stated. "Once we do this we can put really the racket on
the wall and say we did everything we could. But to get to his level, I still
have to work a little bit harder."

For Safina, her meteoric rise to the top of women's tennis also marks her
emergence from her famous brother's shadow. "For some people I will always just be [Marat's] younger sister. But we have completely different

lives. Whatever I have achieved and will achieve, I have done by myself," she noted. "I always wanted to be myself, and now finally the results are coming, and people can know me as Dinara Safina."

HOME AND FAMILY

When she is not traveling on the WTA Tour, Safina makes her home in Monte Carlo, Monaco.

HOBBIES AND OTHER INTERESTS

In her spare time, Safina enjoys going to the movies, reading, and listening to music. She is also a big fan of the European professional soccer team Real Madrid.

HONORS AND AWARDS

U.S. Open, Women's Doubles: 2007
Olympic Tennis, Women's Singles: 2008, silver medal

FURTHER READING

Periodicals

Los Angeles Times, June 3, 2008, p.D3; July 28, 2008, p.D4
New York Times, Sep. 7, 2006, p.D3; Aug. 25, 2008, p.5; Aug. 27, 2008, p.D5
Palm Beach Post, June 5, 2006, p.C10
South Florida Sun-Sentinel, June 6, 2008
Sports Illustrated, June 12, 2006, p.73
USA Today, June 3, 2008, p.C8; June 6, 2008, p.C10

Online Article

http://www.sonyericssonwtatour.com
  (Sony Ericsson WTA Tour, "Ranking Watch: Safina Becomes New No. 2," Oct. 13, 2008)

ADDRESS

Dinara Safina
Sony Ericsson WTA Tour
One Progress Plaza
Suite 1500
St. Petersburg, FL 33701

WORLD WIDE WEB SITES

http://www.dsafina.com
http://www.sonyericssonwtatour.com

Photo and Illustration Credits

Front Cover Photos: Klum: PROJECT RUNWAY Bravo Photo: Virginia Sherwood; Lang Lang: Deutsche Grammophon (Universal Music Group); Lewis: NBC Photo: Margaret Norton; Mallett: FRAZZ © Jef Mallett/Dist. by United Feature Syndicate, Inc. Courtesy Mary Anne Grimes, United Media.

Elizabeth Alexander/Photos: Photo by C. J. Gunther. Courtesy, Elizabeth Alexander (www.elizabethalexander.net) (p. 9); Book Cover: MISS CRANDALL'S SCHOOL FOR YOUNG LADIES & LITTLE MISSES OF COLOR (Wordsong/Boyd Mills Press, Inc.) Text copyright © 2007 by Elizabeth Alexander and Marilyn Nelson. Illustration copyright © 2007 by Floyd Cooper. All Rights Reserved. (p. 11); Ron Edmonds/AP Photo (p. 14).

Michael Cera/Photos: NICK AND NORA'S INFINITE PLAYLIST Photo: Barbara Nitke. © 2008 Playlist LLC. All Rights Reserved. Sony Pictures Entertainment Inc. (p. 19); ROLIE POLIE OLIE: THE GREAT DEFENDER OF FUN. ©Nelvana in Trust ©Disney Enterprises, Inc. All Rights Reserved. (p. 22, top); DVD set: ARRESTED DEVELOPMENT - SEASON ONE. © 2003, 2004 Twentieth Century Fox Film Corporation and Imagine Entertainment. All rights reserved. © 2004 Twentieth Century Fox Home Entertainment, Inc. All Rights Reserved. (p. 22, center); CLARK AND MICHAEL Photo: Monty Brinton/CBS ©2007 CBS Broadcasting Inc. All Rights Reserved. (p. 22, bottom); SUPERBAD © 2007 Columbia Pictures Industries, Inc. All Rights Reserved. Sony Pictures Home Entertainment (p. 25); JUNO © Twentieth Century Fox Film Corporation (p. 26); NICK AND NORA'S INFINITE PLAYLIST Photo: K.C. Bailey © 2008 Playlist LLC. All Rights Reserved. Sony Pictures Entertainment Inc. (p. 28).

Heidi Klum/Photos: PROJECT RUNWAY Bravo Photo: Virginia Sherwood (pp. 31, 37 top); Mike Segar/Reuters/Landov (pp. 33, 40); Rose Hartman/WireImage.com (p. 35); PROJECT RUNWAY Bravo Photo: Barbara Nitke (p. 37, center and bottom).

Lang Lang/Photos: Deutsche Grammophon (Universal Music Group) (p. 45); Book Cover: LANG LANG: PLAYING WITH FLYING KEYS (Delacorte Press/Random House Children's Books) by Lang Lang with Michael French. Text copyright © 2008 by Lang Lang. Photograph © 2008 by Jesse Frohman (p. 48); © Photo: J. Henry Fair/ Deutsche Grammophon (Universal Music Group) (p. 51); CD Cover: HAYDN, RACHMNINOFF, BRAHMS, TCHAIKOVSKY, BALAKIREV/Lang Lang ℗© 2001 TELARC All Rights Reserved. Photo: Christopher Jacobs. Cover design: Anilda Carrasquillo (p. 53); Photo by Tim Hipps, Family and MWR Command. Courtesy U. S. Army (p. 56).

Leona Lewis/Photos: ABC/Adam Larkey (p. 59); Dave Hogan/Getty Images (p. 61); CD cover: SPIRIT © 2008 J Records, a unit of Sony BMG Music Entertainment (p. 64); NBC Photo: Margaret Norton (p. 66).

Jef Mallett/Photos: Kim Kauffman Photography, courtesy Jef Mallett (p. 69); Courtesy Jef Mallett (pp. 70 and 78, left); FRAZZ © Jef Mallett/Dist. by United Feature Syndicate, Inc. Courtesy Mary Anne Grimes, United Media (pp. 72 and 78, right); FRAZZ © Jef Mallett/Dist. by United Feature Syndicate, Inc. (pp. 74, 75); Book cover: FRAZZ: LIVE AT BRYSON ELEMENTARY (Andrew McNeel Publishers) © 2005 by Jef Mallett. All Rights Reserved. (p. 76).

Warith Deen Mohammed/Photos: Stephen J. Carrera, File/AP Photo (p. 81); Hulton Archive/ Getty Images (p. 82); Walter P. Reuther Library, Wayne State University (pp. 85, 87); AP Photo (p. 89); © John Van Hasselt/Corbis Sygma (p. 92); Tim Boyle/Getty Images (p. 95); Danny Johnston/AP Photo (p. 97).

Suze Orman/Photos: © Marc Royce. All Rights Reserved. Courtesy PBS (p. 99); Chris Kleponis/Bloomberg News/Landov (p. 102); Book Cover: YOU'VE EARNED IT, DON'T LOSE IT: MISTAKES YOU CAN'T AFFORD TO MAKE WHEN YOU RETIRE by Suze Orman, with Linda Mead © 1994, 1997, 1998 by Suze Orman. All Rights Reserved. Cover design by Jerry Pfiefer. Author photograph by Kelly Campbell (p. 104); DVD Cover: THE 9 STEPS TO FINANCIAL FREEDOM by Suze Orman. © 1998 Twin Cities Public Television and Q-Direct Ventures Inc. © 2004 Artwork PBS. All Rights Reserved. Photo: Kelly Campbell (p. 106); SATURDAY NIGHT LIVE, NBC Photo: Dana Edelson (p. 109).

Chris Paul/Photos: Bill Haber/AP Photo (p. 115); Linda Spillers/WireImage.com (p. 117); Photo by Brian Westerholt. Courtesy Wake Forest University (p. 120); Phil Ellsworth/ESPN (p. 122); Lucy Nicholson/Reuters/Landov (p. 125); Courtesy USBC (p. 127).

Rachael Ray/Photos: PRNewsFoto via Newscom (pp. 129, 134); Book cover: RACHAEL RAY 30-MINUTE MEALS (Lake Isle Press) © 1998 by Rachael Ray. Photo: Colleen Brescia, courtesy of Food Network. Book design by Ellen Swandiak (p. 132); Peter Kramer/Getty Images (p. 137); PRNewsFoto/Ainsworth Pet Nutrition via Newscom (p. 140).

Emma Roberts/Photos: HOTEL FOR DOGS Photo: Jaimie Trueblood © 2008 DreamWorks LLC and Cold Spring Pictures. All Rights Reserved. (pp. 143 and 152, all photos); DVD: SPYMATE © Buena Vista Entertainment, Inc. All Rights Reserved. (p.146); UNFABULOUS Courtesy of Nickelodeon (p.148); NANCY DREW © 2007 Warner Bros. Entertainment, Inc. All Rights Reserved. Courtesy Warner Home Video (p. 150).

Dinara Safina/Photos: Courtesy adidas (p. 157); Alik Keplicz/AP Photo (p. 159); Francois Mori/AP Photo (p. 161); Charlie Knight/AP Photo (p. 163); Clive Brunskill/Getty Images (p. 166).

Cumulative Names Index

This cumulative index includes the names of all individuals profiled in *Biography Today* since the debut of the series in 1992.

For cumulative general, places of birth, and birthday indexes, please see biographytoday.com.

171

For cumulative general, places of birth, and birthday indexes, please see biographytoday.com.

For cumulative general, places of birth, and birthday indexes, please see biographytoday.com.

173

For cumulative general, places of birth, and birthday indexes, please see biographytoday.com.

175

For cumulative general, places of birth, and birthday indexes, please see biographytoday.com.

For cumulative general, places of birth, and birthday indexes, please see biographytoday.com.

177

For cumulative general, places of birth, and birthday indexes, please see biographytoday.com.

For cumulative general, places of birth, and birthday indexes, please see biographytoday.com.

179

CUMULATIVE NAMES INDEX

Martin, Ricky. . . . . Jan 00
Martinez, Pedro. . . . . Sport V.5
Martinez, Victor . . . . Author V.15
Masih, Iqbal. Jan 96
Mathers, Marshall III
  see Eminem . . . . Apr 03
Mathis, Clint. . . . . Apr 03
Mathison, Melissa . . . . Author V.4
Maxwell, Jody-Anne . . . . Sep 98
Mayer, John. Apr 04
McAdams, Rachel . . . . Apr 06
McCain, John . . . . Apr 00
McCarty, Oseola . . . . Jan 99; Update 99
McCary, Michael
  see Boyz II Men . . . . Jan 96
McClintock, Barbara. . . . . Oct 92
McCloskey, Robert . . . . Author V.15
McCully, Emily Arnold . . Jul 92; Update 93
McDaniel, Lurlene. . . . . Author V.14
McDonald, Janet . . . . Author V.18
McEntire, Reba. . . . . Sep 95
McGrady, Tracy. . . . . Sport V.11
McGrath, Judy . . . . Business V.1
McGruder, Aaron. . . . . Author V.10
McGwire, Mark. . . . . Jan 99; Update 99
McKissack, Fredrick L.. . . . . . . Author V.3
McKissack, Patricia C.. . . . . . . Author V.3
McLean, A.J.
  see Backstreet Boys . . . . Jan 00
McNabb, Donovan . . . . Apr 03
McNair, Steve . . . . Sport V.11
McNutt, Marcia . . . . Science V.11
Mead, Margaret . . . . Science V.2
Meaker, Marijane
  see Kerr, M.E.. . . . . Author V.1
Mebarak Ripoll, Shakira Isabel
  see Shakira . . . . PerfArt V.1
Meissner, Kimmie. . . . . Sep 08
Meltzer, Milton. . . . . Author V.11
Memmel, Chellsie. . . . . Sport V.14
Menchu, Rigoberta. . . . . Jan 93
Mendes, Chico . . . . WorLdr V.1
Messier, Mark . . . . Apr 96
Michalka, Alyson Renae
  see Aly & AJ. . . . . Sep 08
Michalka, Amanda Joy
  see Aly & AJ. . . . . Sep 08
Milbrett, Tiffeny . . . . Sport V.10
Millan, Cesar . . . . Sep 06

Miller, Percy Romeo
  see Romeo, Lil' . . . . Jan 06
Miller, Rand . . . . Science V.5
Miller, Robyn. . . . . Science V.5
Miller, Shannon. . . . . Sep 94; Update 96
Milosevic, Slobodan . . . Sep 99; Update 00; Update 01; Update 02
Mirra, Dave . . . . Sep 02
Mister Rogers
  see Rogers, Fred. . . . . PerfArt V.3
Mitchell-Raptakis, Karen . . . . Jan 05
Mittermeier, Russell A.. . . . . . . WorLdr V.1
Miyamoto, Shigeru . . . . Science V.5
Mobutu Sese Seko . . WorLdr V.2; Update 97
Moceanu, Dominique . . . . Jan 98
Mohajer, Dineh. . . . . Jan 02
Mohammed, Warith Deen . . . . . . Apr 09
Monroe, Bill . . . . Sep 97
Montana, Joe . . . . Jan 95; Update 95
Moore, Henry. . . . . Artist V.1
Moore, Mandy. . . . . Jan 04
Moreno, Arturo R.. . . . . Business V.1
Morgan, Garrett. . . . . Science V.2
Morissette, Alanis . . . . Apr 97
Morita, Akio. . . . . Science V.4
Morris, Nathan
  see Boyz II Men . . . . Jan 96
Morris, Wanya
  see Boyz II Men . . . . Jan 96
Morrison, Lillian . . . . Author V.12
Morrison, Samuel . . . . Sep 97
Morrison, Toni . . . . Jan 94
Moseley, Jonny . . . . Sport V.8
Moses, Grandma. . . . . Artist V.1
Moss, Cynthia . . . . WorLdr V.3
Moss, Randy. . . . . Sport V.4
Mother Teresa
  see Teresa, Mother . . . . Apr 98
Mowat, Farley. . . . . Author V.8
Mugabe, Robert . . . . WorLdr V.2
Muhammad, Wallace Delaney
  see Mohammed, Warith Dean . . . . Apr 09
Muir, John . . . . WorLdr V.3
Muldowney, Shirley . . . . Sport V.7
Muniz, Frankie . . . . Jan 01
Murie, Margaret . . . . WorLdr V.1
Murie, Olaus J. . . . . WorLdr V.1
Murphy, Eddie . . . . PerfArt V.2
Murphy, Jim . . . . Author V.17
Murray, Ty . . . . Sport V.7

For cumulative general, places of birth, and birthday indexes, please see biographytoday.com.

For cumulative general, places of birth, and birthday indexes, please see biographytoday.com.

181

For cumulative general, places of birth, and birthday indexes, please see biographytoday.com.

For cumulative general, places of birth, and birthday indexes, please see biographytoday.com.

183

For cumulative general, places of birth, and birthday indexes, please see biographytoday.com.

185

Biography Today

General Series

B*iography Today* **General Series** includes a unique combination of current biographical profiles that teachers and librarians — and the readers themselves — tell us are most appealing. The **General Series** is available as a 3-issue subscription; hardcover annual cumulation; or subscription plus cumulation.

Within the **General Series**, your readers will find a variety of sketches about:

- Authors
- Musicians
- Political leaders
- Sports figures
- Movie actresses & actors
- Cartoonists
- Scientists
- Astronauts
- TV personalities
- and the movers & shakers in many other fields!

"*Biography Today* will be useful in elementary and middle school libraries and in public library children's collections where there is a need for biographies of current personalities. High schools serving reluctant readers may also want to consider a subscription."
— *Booklist,* American Library Association

"Highly recommended for the young adult audience. Readers will delight in the accessible, energetic, tell-all style; teachers, librarians, and parents will welcome the clever format [and] intelligent and informative text. It should prove especially useful in motivating 'reluctant' readers or literate nonreaders."
— *MultiCultural Review*

"Written in a friendly, almost chatty tone, the profiles offer quick, objective information. While coverage of current figures makes *Biography Today* a useful reference tool, an appealing format and wide scope make it a fun resource to browse." — *School Library Journal*

"<u>The</u> best source for current information at a level kids can understand."
— Kelly Bryant, School Librarian, Carlton, OR

"Easy for kids to read. We love it! Don't want to be without it."
— Lynn McWhirter, School Librarian, Rockford, IL

ONE-YEAR SUBSCRIPTION
- 3 softcover issues, 6" x 9"
- Published in January, April, and September
- 1-year subscription, list price $66. **School and library price $64**
- 150 pages per issue
- 10 profiles per issue
- Contact sources for additional information
- Cumulative Names Index

HARDBOUND ANNUAL CUMULATION
- Sturdy 6" x 9" hardbound volume
- Published in December
- List price $73. **School and library price $66 per volume**
- 450 pages per volume
- 30 profiles — includes all profiles found in softcover issues for that calendar year
- Cumulative General Index, Places of Birth Index, and Birthday Index

SUBSCRIPTION AND CUMULATION COMBINATION
- $110 for 3 softcover issues plus the hardbound volume

For Cumulative General, Places of Birth, and Birthday Indexes, please see www.biographytoday.com.